THE REAL YOU:
BEYOND FORMS AND LIVES

Irmansyah Effendi, M.Sc.

BALBOA.
PRESS
A DIVISION OF HAY HOUSE

Balboa Press books may be ordered through booksellers or by contacting:

Balboa Press
A Division of Hay House
1663 Liberty Drive
Bloomington, IN 47403
www.balboapress.com
1-(877) 407-4847

ISBN: 978-1-4525-5384-9 (sc)
ISBN: 978-1-4525-5386-3 (hc)
ISBN: 978-1-4525-5385-6 (e)

Library of Congress Control Number: 2012913740

Because of the dynamic nature of the Internet, any web addresses or links contained in this book may have changed since publication and may no longer be valid. The views expressed in this work are solely those of the author and do not necessarily reflect the views of the publisher, and the publisher hereby disclaims any responsibility for them.

The author of this book does not dispense medical advice or prescribe the use of any technique as a form of treatment for physical, emotional, or medical problems without the advice of a physician, either directly or indirectly. The intent of the author is only to offer information of a general nature to help you in your quest for emotional and spiritual well-being. In the event you use any of the information in this book for yourself, which is your constitutional right, the author and the publisher assume no responsibility for your actions.

Printed in the United States of America

Balboa Press rev. date: 08/17/2012

May All Beings Prioritize True Source (The Creator) More.

Contents

List of Illustrations

Preface

The topic of who we really are/our spirit/true self is not new to many people as it has been mentioned in various holy books, yet, not too many people know their real selves. To some people, finding out about their true self is very important: many of them spend much of their time trying to find information about true self, and some have spent decades traveling the world to gain insight from various perspectives. There are various reasons why people feel that it is important to find out about their true self. For instance, some want to achieve authentic happiness in life while others have some spiritual purposes such as believing that only by knowing about their true self can they know about the Creator. Many others, however, do not feel the need to find out about their true self because they see it as strange or even scary.

This book gives clear, simple information about our true self. Regardless of how much one knows about true self, there is something for everyone in this book. Those with no prior knowledge about true self will find the information about what true self is and the connection between true self and our physical body easy to understand. Those who have been seeking will find clarification on what it is that they are looking for and how to find what they are looking for. May all readers use the information on true self just to surrender to the Source of true selves/ True Source/the Creator.

For a little more than a decade, I have been dedicating my life helping others to realize for themselves this higher consciousness within themselves. Having helped thousands of people to remember about their true selves and the journey of their true selves, and having reached true self consciousness myself gave me a broader perspective and deeper realizations about true self, which I share with you in this book.

Everything I share in this book is not a result of mere contemplation or unnatural techniques. Not at all. The realizations that I gained about true self consciousness is obtained through Inner Heart, the real spark of True Source that realizes True Source's Will. In reaching true self consciousness, there is no technique; it is all about relying on True Source's Blessing. In this book, you will see clearly that everything is really about relying on True Source's Blessing. After all, everything is only a beautiful facility to surrender more to True Source.

In addition to <u>The Real You: Beyond Forms and Lives</u> book, where I explain what true self is, the differences between the soul and spirit/ true self, the connection between true self and physical body, and how all this information can be used to live this life, my <u>Spiritual Journey for the Ultimate Destiny</u> book will help you complete the picture. Understanding your true self and your spiritual journey will give meaning to your life. Your daily activities will become beautiful and meaningful as you go on your spiritual journey in this life.

May this book remind us why we are on this earth and may all the information be used the best just so we can rely on True Source's Blessing and surrender with an open heart to True Source.

Chapter 1

INTRODUCTION

When I was young, I would read holy books, and I often came across the term 'spirit' or 'true self.' However, back then, I thought that spirit was something deep within us that we could not possibly know about while we were still alive on this earth. I did, however, feel that somehow our spirit was affected by our attitude and condition while we were still alive.

In a way, what I thought of about our true self was both right and wrong. Before I explain further, I will tell you my "meetings" related to stories about true self.

After my graduate studies in the U.S.A., I returned to Indonesia and studied meditation from the late Mr. Ammirudin. He would tell me stories about true self, and it was clear from the way he was telling the stories that matters related to the spirit/true self were important. However, because of my limited understanding back then, I was fascinated by the stories themselves instead of the meaning or the main message of these stories, which was about true self.

Mr. Ammirudin told me about his meeting with an American professor who spent more than a decade traveling the world to learn about his own true self because he knew that getting to know his own true self was crucial in his spiritual journey/spiritual progress. Mr. Ammirudin told me that after doing a certain exercise, the professor was able to see his own true self in a mirror.

In addition to Mr. Ammirudin's story about the professor, another teacher of mine also shared with me his own personal experience. He told me about how he had spent 50 years learning about spirituality and how he was able to go to higher dimensions. According to him, in one very high dimension, beings there did not have the lower part of their bodies because the lower part of the body was the center of lust and desires. Without the lower part of the body, there was no lust or desire.

Hearing these fascinating stories impressed me, but I still did not really understand why these people were looking for their true selves and would want to go through all kinds of experiences. I also did not understand why in telling me all these stories, my teachers' mannerism and attitude showed very clearly that spirit/true self was very important.

Years later, I read many spiritual books, and some of these books talked about our true self. They often mentioned "the self within us," "the perfect self," "the all-knowing self," and other statements about true self. Many of the writers considered true self as the spark of the Creator, and this was the reason why true self knew everything and was even perfect. The writers also claimed that when we obtained information from our true self, everything would become easy. Some of them even believed that when a person reached his/her true self's consciousness, spiritually he/she was near perfection.

In addition to claiming that true self was perfect and the benefits of getting information from true self, many of the writers talked about how to make a connection with true self. They call the method of communicating with true self "channeling." In channeling, one would contemplate about a topic and would write down whatever comes to mind. This information would be considered information from a higher consciousness or even from true self. Indeed, there are many interesting stories about channeling.

The books also talked about methods people employed to reach their true self consciousness. One common method was hypnosis, and another through trance. I personally felt that something was not right with hypnosis or trance. Later on, after I realized the differences between the soul and the spirit (true self), I understood that there was a mix-up and a misunderstanding about the soul and true self by those who used hypnosis and trance to reach their true self consciousness.

In the meantime, as I was practicing meditation routinely, my Kundalini was awakened spontaneously without proper preparation. I experienced Kundalini syndrome, looked for help, and after my

Kundalini problems were taken care of, I started meeting nonphysical teachers. One of my nonphysical teachers taught me about Shing Chi (detailed information can be read in my Shing Chi book). I then started practicing Shing Chi, Kundalini, soul consciousness, and other spiritual exercises until I completed them all. Yet, even with all that fast progress, I felt that I was still behind a huge wall. There were still many spiritual matters that I did not understand.

A part of me felt that the next step was to reach my true self consciousness, but I had no clear reference on how I could reach this true self consciousness even after I looked everywhere and read all kinds of books including those in psychology and other fields.

Years later, after I changed the type of exercises that I did, i.e. moving away from Kundalini, Shing Chi, and other spiritual exercises to remembering True Source's Blessings and starting to rely on True Source's Blessings, it was True Source's Blessings that helped me reach my true self consciousness.

Reaching my true self consciousness was the next step of my spiritual journey. As a true self, I witnessed many things that were unclear and were questioned by many people. I began to realize that the things that I read and knew about (that were considered common knowledge in the spiritual world) were actually very limited.

The realizations that I obtained about so many things were no longer based on merely peeking or looking at these things from afar but were from a firsthand experience as a true self. For example, I was able to see that the knowledge obtained from "channeling" was not completely correct. Through channeling, one tends to be connected to one's subconsciousness instead of the true self consciousness which was the highest consciousness. Channeling did not even connect someone to the mediator consciousness, which was the soul, a consciousness higher than our daily consciousness, the brain (more information on this is in Soul Consciousness).

Through firsthand experience as true self, my understanding about True Source's Love changed, and this was a very important and valuable realization. I saw clearly how what the books said about the Creator being busy taking care of many things and therefore the Creator gave us "toys" in the form of paranormal abilities to keep us occupied was not true. Some books also said that the Creator was too busy to even listen to our call. As a true self, I saw clearly how untrue all this was.

The Creator definitely does not give us toys to keep us occupied because there are other matters to be taken care of. The Creator/the Source of our true self loves us completely, and to True Source, nothing is impossible and everything can be done easily. It is us who need to let go of all of the "toys." We are the ones who are busy with our desires, busyness, and our own ways, and this is what prevents us from accepting True Source's Love. We are the ones who need to remember the real purpose of our lives. We need to continue to call out to the Source of our true self/True Source with our heart directed to the True Source, letting True Source take care of us completely.

As a true self, I also saw very clearly how many humans and other beings, when praying to the Creator, do not use their hearts well enough. In addition, many beings pray to the Creator only for their own needs or desires; to them, praying is like reading a shopping list.

With the change of my understanding of True Source's Love as a result of what I had witnessed and realized as true self, I decided to let go all that I knew, even if the knowledge contained *some* truth. I realize now that I need true knowledge, and it is better to have one piece of knowledge that is 100% true rather than having 100 pieces of knowledge that are not 100% true because everything affects our attitude and our direction. I do not want to hold on to knowledge that is contaminated and have my attitude and direction be contaminated.

With this attitude, I stopped practicing to get something, and I started to open my heart and to surrender to the Creator/True Source. The more I open my heart and surrender to True Source, the more I realize how True Source is indeed the Most Loving.

It is obvious that it is us who are too busy with our own desires and our own ways, to the point where we do not even remember True Source, or when we do remember True Source, it is only for our needs and desires again. Even in communicating with True Source when we do remember True Source, we use our own ways instead of using our heart, the special Gift of Love from True Source that is the key connection to True Source.

Because our heart is the key connection to True Source, I invited others to strengthen their hearts and open their hearts to True Source through Strengthening of the Heart exercise and Open Heart Prayer. Both Strengthening of the Heart exercise and Open Heart Prayer are not techniques to get anything except to rely on and surrender more to True Source. Strengthening of the Heart exercise connects us to our heart naturally and strengthens our heart and the beautiful feeling from our heart. Open Heart Prayer is a prayer that relies on True Source's Blessings to cleanse our heart from the negativities that we create ourselves because of negative emotions such as anger, arrogance, envy, jealousy, sadness, disappointment and so on that are very much present in humans' lives. Every time we experience negative emotions, we create negativities, and we send out these negativities to our surrounding, and we dirty our heart. We cannot cleanse our heart. Only True Source can cleanse our heart. No other being can touch or affect our heart. This is why our heart is special. Opening our heart to True Source means we are letting True Source cleanse, open, direct, and do the most beautiful and wonderful things to our heart.

Using my heart frequently, I can feel that my connection to True Source changes beautifully. Now, every time I pray, I am able to feel True Source's Unlimited Love that True Source gives abundantly, and my heart is filled with the beauty of the Love and much joy.

Another very important realization that I obtained was about our heart's and true self's limitation. Through my experience of helping others reach their true self consciousness, I saw how even though everyone saw and experienced the same thing as true selves, each had different understandings. I initially thought that only our brain was limited and that true self consciousness, being the highest consciousness of ours, was not limited. The different perceptions over the same truths by different true selves who go through the same experiences show clearly how our true selves are just like our limited brain.

Upon my realization that even our highest consciousness was limited, I prayed and prayed to True Source, asking for guidance. I was given the realization that true self is still learning; this is why we are on this earth. If our true selves were perfect, we would not be here. We are here for our true self to learn.

Knowing that we are limited and that we can have different perceptions of the same truths should help us see even more clearly that we need to follow not our true self but the core of our heart and the core of our true self, which is the spark of True Source: our Inner Heart. None of our consciousnesses (brain, soul, or true self) is perfect. We are far from perfect. We are still learning. We do not know what is proper or the best. Our Inner Heart, the spark of True Source, is the only one that can realize real truths. Instead of relying on our brain or even our true self, we need to have our Inner Heart be the director.

Having our Inner Heart as the director should answer many people's question about why our true self, the highest consciousness, must be given two lower consciousnesses, i.e. soul consciousness and brain consciousness. How can our true self learn from a much lower consciousness such as our brain?

The realization that the spark of True Source should be the director reminds us again that we need to follow only our Inner Heart and not our true self. We do not need to waste our time trying to find out what our true self knows. We do not need to wonder any longer why our highest consciousnesses still needs two lower consciousnesses: it is clear that the purpose of the soul consciousness and the brain consciousness is to help our imperfect true self to learn. Even our lowest consciousness, our brain, is a beautiful facility given by True Source to help us to remember about our Inner Heart and to use Inner Heart so that all of our consciousnesses, including our true self can learn to use Inner Heart.

The emphasis that our Inner Heart is a spark of True Source is NOT to compare our Inner Heart with True Source. Not at all. Although our Inner Heart is a spark of True Source, it is like a speck of dust. The emphasis that Inner Heart is a spark of True Source is only to remind us that only the spark can connect with the Creator. No other parts of us, especially not the flesh and blood part (our brain) can realize the Will of the Creator's the way the spark can realize it. I am giving this explanation because a participant in an Inner Heart workshop asked me whether this was about comparing ourselves to the Creator. Not at all. In the intermediate level of my workshops, I invite people to "witness" the experiences of other true selves by using their Inner Heart and their Heart so that they can start recognizing many things about true self and our connection with True Source. In the higher level of the workshops, everyone is given the opportunity to rely onto the Blessings to reach true self consciousness (to realize themselves as true selves).

I have been helping many people all around the world to reach their true self consciousness simply by relying on True Source's Blessings to surrender more to True Source. I understand some people are concerned about true self because holy books talk about true self yet at the same time say that information about true self is limited by the Creator. Everything I share in this book is not a reading report based on other people's writing but is based on my own experience and the experience of thousands of people I have helped in reaching true self consciousness just to surrender more to the Creator. Those I helped in reaching their true self consciousness and I myself used our Inner Hearts to reach our true self consciousness, and it was possible only because of the Creator's Blessing as we rely solely on the Creator. If the Creator does not want us to know certain matters, obviously we will not know about these matters. Things that we are not supposed to know will not be shown to our Inner Heart.

This book will start with an explanation of what true self is as well as the two lower consciousnesses. I ask that you distance yourself first from everything that you have ever known about true self while reading this book so that you can read the information here in detail and to please remember that the information here is not a theory or a summary of various literatures read.

The main discussion in this book is about the connection between our true self and us as a whole being with the Creator. You will understand why our true self was given this limited physical body that can get sick, get tired, and can die. We need to have this understanding so that we can live our life the best, according to the real purpose of life. Some of you may be disappointed because I will not talk about fascinating matters even though many people and I have reached our true self consciousness and have realized these matters very clearly. This is done purposely so that you are not busy comparing your own experiences related to your own true self as things that look similar can actually be very different.

No matter what your knowledge is in regard to true self, hopefully this book can give you an understanding of what true self is, just to understand the real purpose of life and to use this life the best simply by surrendering to the Creator.

Chapter 2

HUMANS' THREE CONSCIOUSNESSES

In our daily life, most of us are very familiar with the outermost part of ourselves: our physical body with our brain as the center of consciousness. Actually, humans have three consciousnesses:

o   spirit/true self consciousness
o   soul consciousness
o   physical consciousness (brain)

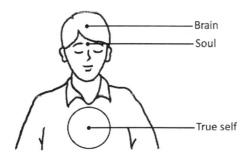

Illustration 1: human's three consciousnesses

Spirit/True Self Consciousness

Spirit or true self consciousness is often times referred to as the spark of the Creator. True Self refers to who we really are that has been in existence for a very long time and will continue to exist after the other parts of us vanish. It is often said that the other parts of us are just layers. A common analogy is that the other parts of us are just the clothing for our true self. Information on true self will be elaborated in this whole book.

Soul Consciousness

I do not use the terms "soul" and "spirit" the way these words are commonly used or understood by many people. The way these two words are used in this book may even be the opposite of how they are used by many people. This is not because I want to create something new or because I want to be different.

I use the term "spirit" to refer to the spark of the Creator; this is why it feels right to see our spirit as our true self. "Soul," on the other hand, is the mediator between true self and our physical body. More complete information on the soul can be read in my <u>Soul Consciousness</u> book. For now, the discussion on the terminology serves to show that true self consciousness is not the same as soul consciousness.

Our limited true self needs a facility to learn; this is why the Creator gave us a physical body. However, the difference between our physical body and our true self is so great that we need a mediator for them—this is our soul consciousness.

Our soul consciousness:

1. functions as a mediator
2. archives our experiences.

1. Soul: A Mediator

Because our true self and our physical body are very different from each other, and the difference is too great, an intermediary medium is needed, and this comes in the form of non-physical body layers whose center of consciousness is the soul.

2. Soul: An Archive of Experiences

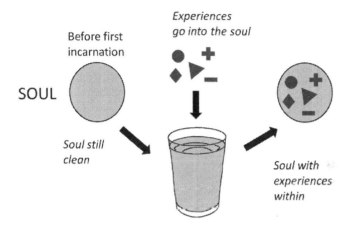

Illustration 2: soul: archiving experiences

Our soul along with the non-physical body layers functions as an archive for all of our experiences. In the belief of reincarnations, these non-physical body layers and the soul keep a record and continue to carry all of the experiences throughout all incarnations.

We need the soul and the non-physical body layers to keep these experiences because none of the interactions or consequences that took place in life are kept by true self because true self is beyond all dimensions. True self only obtains realizations from all the experiences the physical form goes through.

The non-physical layers and the soul are not eternal because just like our physical body, these layers are only "layers" or "clothing"; they are not who we really are. We have heard stories about seeing the form of a person who has passed on that looks very much like the physical form when the person was still alive. This is the non-physical body layer whose center of consciousness is the soul.

Brain Consciousness

Our brain is the center of our physical consciousness, and in our daily life, we use it all the time. We clearly use our brain every waking moment. Also, albeit minimal, we actually use our brain too when we sleep.

The table below shows the connection between our physical body and the rest of our consciousnesses and where each one is located.

Consciousness	Form	Explanation
Physical consciousness (our brain)	our physical body	the outermost layer
Soul consciousness	6 non-physical body layers (layer 2 to layer 7)	in between physical and true self consciousness
True self consciousness	no form	often times considered to be the deepest when actually there is still Inner Heart in the very core

Chapter 3

CONSCIOUSNESSES

When I use the term "consciousness," I am not referring to the *form* of us but to the *center* of consciousness of that related part of us instead. The center of consciousness of our physical body is our brain. The center of consciousness of our non-physical body layers is our soul. The center of consciousness of our true self is our true self.

The Relationships among the Three Consciousnesses

Illustration 3a: *layers of consciousnesses in humans*, shows the connection among the three consciousnesses in a human. Within a physical body, there is always a soul. Within a soul, there is always true self. In a human, the soul cannot possibly exist without true self. At the core of all this is Inner Heart. Our true self cannot possibly exist without Inner Heart.

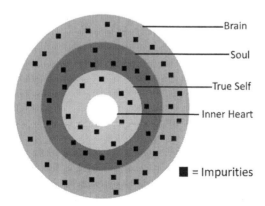

Illustration 3a: layers of consciousnesses in humans

Our physical body and the center of its consciousness are the outermost layer and the coarsest of all of our consciousnesses. This physical consciousness is often referred to as normal consciousness or daily consciousness. Our soul consciousness and our true self consciousness are our higher consciousnesses. The soul is the "intermediate" higher consciousness and true self consciousness is the highest level of consciousness.

The black dots in Illustration 3a represent impurities and negativities that are present in each level of consciousnesses, including in true self consciousness. Only Inner Heart, the spark of the Creator, which is the core of all consciousnesses, is pure.

From the illustration, it is clear that in humans, the physical consciousness (the brain) is the outermost layer, and it covers everything else inside it. Although soul consciousness and true self consciousness are aware of what is going on, it is the brain that interacts directly with the surroundings. In general, the two higher consciousnesses (soul and true self) do not get a chance to directly interact with the physical surroundings unless the ideas or desires from these consciousnesses are followed by the human.

As soon as a human dies, the center of the physical consciousness, i.e. the brain, vanishes too. The soul consciousness, with true self within it, becomes the outermost layer. Unlike the brain that thinks, soul and true self do not need to think at all in order to function. This is why I do not use the term "center of thoughts" but "center of consciousnesses"—the brain is the only one that thinks; soul and true self are non physical; they do not need to think.

Illustration 3b shows the layers of consciousnesses after death. As soon as a human dies, the soul, containing and carrying all of life experiences including the consequences from past actions, is now the outermost layer and is the one interacting with the surroundings.

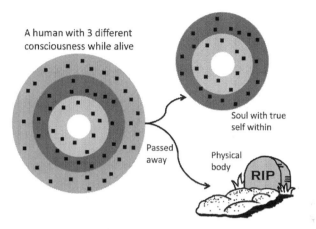

A human with 3 different consciousness while alive

Soul with true self within

Passed away

Physical body

RIP

Illustration 3b: layers of consciousnesses upon death

Few people are aware of the connection among these three consciousnesses in humans. Even the term 'soul' and 'spirit' are still being used interchangeably; this is precisely because the difference between the two is unknown to many.

Knowing the difference between the soul and the spirit is not just about clarifying terminology. This understanding is crucial to the attainment of the purpose of life. You will notice that stories about the soul are usually stories related to heaven and hell while stories about spirit are related to returning to True Source. Knowing the difference between the soul and the spirit should clarify whether the real purpose of life is to go to heaven/hell or to return to the Creator/True Source. Only when we return to True Source completely can we enjoy True Source's Love forever. Nothing else is eternal.

Subconsciousness is NOT a Higher Consciousness

You may have noticed that I did not mention subconsciousness when explaining human consciousnesses. Subconsciousness is another terminology that is sometimes used interchangeably with other consciousnesses by many people (including myself a decade ago).

Many people use the term subconsciousness to refer to any consciousness that is outside of the daily consciousness. In other words, subconsciousness is thought of just like soul consciousness or true self consciousness when actually soul and true self consciousnesses are higher consciousnesses while subconsciousness is only a waste-collection place.

Subconsciousness simply collects waste from the brain, soul, and true self consciousnesses.

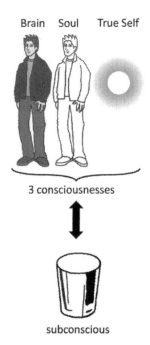

Illustration 4: the three consciousnesses and subconsciousness

Again, soul consciousness and true self consciousness are consciousnesses that are higher than the normal/daily/physical consciousness (our brain) while subconsciousness is a collection of waste from human's three consciousnesses. The misunderstanding and misuse of the terms is caused by the lack of understanding of what "higher consciousness" means. This is also why when people see others who are connected to the subconsciousness and speak of matters outside of the brain capacity, they immediately assume that these people are in their higher consciousness.

There is a very simple way to tell whether someone is in his/her higher consciousness properly or whether he/she is in his/her subconsciousness. In addition to having information that his/her brain cannot possibly know, a person who is in his/her higher consciousness should still be aware of his/her daily surroundings. He/she still knows where he/she is, the day, the date, his/her name, and other normal/daily situations. Also, a person in a higher consciousness has a consistent and controlled behavior. Reaching a higher consciousness does not mean losing daily consciousness.

Therefore, clearly, people who are under hypnosis, in a trance, or in any other techniques where they are not aware of their daily surroundings are not connected to their higher consciousness. At any time a person loses his/her daily consciousness while experiencing something outside of the daily consciousness, he/she is connected to his/her subconsciousness.

> "... those under hypnosis, in a trance, or in any other techniques where they are not aware of their daily surroundings are not connected to their higher consciousness."

Reaching Higher Consciousnesses

To many people, reaching a higher consciousness properly is not easy. Many people have spent years or even decades in trying to reach their higher consciousness. Reaching a higher consciousness properly is actually simple when you are guided by someone who knows how to really do it properly. If you open your heart and use your heart properly, you will start experiencing some sort of higher consciousness even if it is not complete yet. By using your heart properly, your daily consciousness continues to function, and as your heart starts to function too, your heart gives you realizations that your brain cannot give you. Using your heart completely is not really the same as reaching a higher consciousness, but at least you can start to realize things from your heart while your brain continues to function properly.

Chapter 4

THE REAL US: TRUE SELF (SPIRIT)

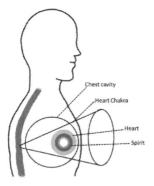

Illustration 5a: True Self within Our Heart

True self or spirit is also known as a "higher self," "super-consciousness," "supra-consciousness," "atman," and so on. In Smile to Your Heart Meditations book, I explained about our true self located inside the chest cavity, within our heart. Obviously the heart we are talking about is the nonphysical heart which cannot be found in any physical-anatomy book. Our heart is the key connection to True Source—our heart is the one that can connect us humans with the Creator because the physical part of us is only flesh and blood that will become dust at the end of this physical life. It is our true self that resides within our heart—a spark of the the True Source—that can communicate with True Source, not any other parts of us. For those of you who have read my Inner Heart book, I also explained that it is not our whole true self that is a spark of the True Source's, but the core of our true self, our Inner Heart, is the spark of the True Source.

In holy books, we hear about how our true self/spirit is given to us to bring us to life, and many people ask: "Why are we given a spirit by the Creator?" From this question, it is clear that the "we" refers to the humans that we know as ourselves today. According to this human version of the story, the Creator blesses us by giving us a true self so that we could come to life when actually our physical body along with its consciousness is the one that is "new" and "temporary." The physical body that we know of is only some decades old; this is why it can be considered new. It is temporary because it does not last long (most of us do not even live up to 100 years old). Our true self, on the other hand, has been in existence long before we were in our mother's womb and will continue to be in existence even after we have died. Thus, instead of thinking that our spirit was given to us, it is more accurate to say that our physical body was given to our spirit/our true self by True Source.

Our true self, which has been in existence long before this physical body, is the true self consciousness that is not limited like our physical consciousness. Our true self knows a lot of things that our brain is incapable of knowing. Our true self has information from a long span of time from many dimensions, even beyond dimensions because it does not forget. However, always remember: our true self is not perfect yet; this is why we are given this life with this physical body; our true self needs to learn/realize something important through living this limited, physical life.

It is very important to always remember that even though our true self knows a lot of things, it is not perfect and that our physical body is given to our true self in order for it to learn and realize something important. Without this understanding, we may try all kinds of things to access information from our true self, wasting our time and even our life for this purpose. As impressive as it sounds because our true self indeed knows much more than what our brain knows, the information is actually information from our own true self. If our true self already has all this information/knowledge all along even before we were born into this life, for sure our life is not to be used to discover what we ourselves have already known all along. Even if we discover all of the knowledge from our true self, if we do not discover what it is that we actually need to learn, we are back to square one, back to where we were in the first place, regardless of the hard work we have done to access the information that our true self has.

This is why we need to know what our true self needs to learn/realize. Why are we given this life with this body and brain that are very limited compared to our true self? By knowing why we are here, we can start living our life for the real purpose.

Also, to remind ourselves again, although our true self knows a lot of things, it is far from perfect. Only our Inner Heart, the core of our true self, as the spark of the Creator is pure. Thus, instead of looking for information from our true self, we need to listen to our Inner Heart because not only does our Inner Heart give us the correct information all the time, but our Inner Heart also always shows us things that are according to True Source's Will.

Inner Heart is the core of our true self. Illustration 5b shows Inner Heart within our true self along with the other two parts of our true self.

1. Inner Heart: the core of true self; the spark of True Source
2. Sir: the layer around Inner Heart. When someone has an access behind Sir/has access to Inner Heart, he/she will know a lot of things that to most people are secrets.*
3. Realizations/understanding: the outermost part of true self. This part shows the development of one's true self (someone's spiritual progress).

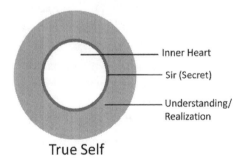

True Self

Illustration 5b: parts of true self

*Though "sir" means "secret," using our Inner Heart is always safe. As a matter of fact, using our Inner Heart is the safest way because only True Source's Blessings can touch our heart and our true self, and only with True Source's Blessings can we realize things from our Inner Heart. If the information that we want to know is not allowed, we will not be able to know it. In other words, by using and following our Inner Heart, we will not go against True Source's Will; this is very important and such joy. Our Inner Heart is very special. With our brain and because of our strong desires, it is very possible for us to mistake things as good and learn these things when actually they are against True Source's Will. Our Inner Heart, however, does not go against True Source's Will.

The following are several basic things about our true self:

o   true self is a part of us at all times
u   true self is not strange/a foreign object
o   we do not need to look for our true self
o   true self is beyond physical and beyond nonphysical
o   true self is very old
o   true self was not given to the human that we are today; rather, our physical form was the one given to our true self by True Source.

True Self: a Part of Us at All Times

Regardless of our belief (whether we believe every human has a true self/whether or not we remember we have true self or not), we do have a true self. True self cannot be separated from human. Without true self, there is no human.

We have to remember that this physical body is temporary: it came into existence when we were in the womb, and it will cease to exist upon our death. Our true self, on the other hand, has been in existence long before we were formed in the womb and continues to exist even after we die.

True Self: Not a Strange Thing/a Foreign Object

Our true self is not a strange/foreign object. How we are today (our human attitude and characteristics) reflects the attitude and characteristics of our true self (albeit not completely because we have three consciousnesses and the dominance of each consciousness depends on each of us). I noticed that many people tried very hard to find out about their true self when actually it is a part of us at all times and therefore is not a strange/foreign object.

True Self: No Need to Search for It

Since our true self is always a part of us at all times, we do not need to search for it. We are our true self even though we are not able to directly realize it because that part of us is within the soul and the brain. Not searching for our true self will serve as a good foundation for us to be able to get to know our true self further.

True Self: Beyond Physical and Beyond Nonphysical

The term "non physical matters" is often used to refer to things that cannot be seen by our physical eyes. Obviously this is an oversimplified definition since there are other forms that we consider belonging to the physical realm even though our eyes cannot see them. For example, the air and gases are examples of physical matters; it just so happens that we cannot see them with our physical eyes.

Non-physical matters are not as simple as many people think. There are 365 dimensions in the whole existence, and in each dimension, matters within it vibrate at certain frequency. The earth and the rest of the planets in our solar system, even our galaxy along with the other galaxies, vibrate in a certain frequency that allows them to be visible to our physical eyes; thus, we call these physical matters. In other dimensions, matters vibrate at frequencies different from the physical dimension. You may have heard about humans' nonphysical body layers. There are six nonphysical body layers in addition to our physical body. Each layer of the nonphysical body is actually in a different dimension. Of course, just because we have seven body layers does not mean that there are only seven dimensions in the whole existence. There are learning dimensions and other dimensions beyond.

Our dimension is often known as the third dimension as it is located the third from the bottom in the 365 learning dimensions. Outside of our physical dimension, all other dimensions are nonphysical. In addition to these learning dimensions, there are other special dimensions above and below them.

True self, True Source's Blessings, and other related divine matters are not in one of these 365 dimensions but beyond all these dimensions. This is why even though true self is not physical, I do not consider it nonphysical either because it is beyond nonphysical. Some people even categorize true self as something divine.

Illustration 6a shows the common perception of how realms are divided into physical realm and nonphysical realm, with divine matters being considered as a part of the nonphysical realm. This is a common misconception.

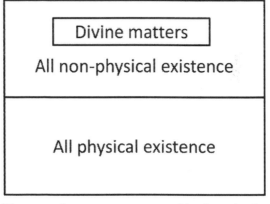

Illustration 6a: common perception of the physical realm, nonphysical realm, and Divine Matters

True self cannot be seen or understood by clairvoyance (the ability to see nonphysical matters) because true self is beyond all these dimensions, and true self does not have a form. Illustration 6b shows that divine matters are not a part of the nonphysical realm as widely believed by people. Instead, divine matters are beyond the nonphysical realm (detailed information on dimensions can be read in <u>Spiritual Journey for the Ultimate Destiny</u>). In order to recognize and understand true self, we need to use our heart and of course the core of our heart, our Inner Heart.

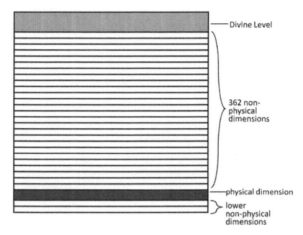

Illustration 6b: the real physical realm, non-physical realm, and Divine Matters

True Self is Very Old.

As previously mentioned, our true self has been in existence for a long time. Our true self is very old, but our true self's age is not a topic to be discussed in this book because finding out about this matter through reading is limited knowledge. The best is to realize it using our own Inner Heart.

Our physical body was not given a spirit; our spirit was given a physical body.

As humans, we read from holy books that our spirit was placed in our body, giving us life. From this human perspective, we are given a true self. The truth is, our true self has been in existence before our human form came into existence. Our physical body was not given a spirit; rather, our spirit was given a physical body.

Other Matters

Below is additional information about what our true self looks like and what/who our true self really is.

1. The Form of Our True Self

We label many forms of matters based on their elements. Because true self is not a physical matter yet it is beyond nonphysical, we actually do not have a label for true self. Some people use the term "light" to refer to the form of true self while others use the term "spark" to refer to the form of true self that is beyond any other matters that we know of.

A true self that has opened its heart, chooses the Creator, and is directed towards the Creator is not only closer to the Creator but is also brighter and cleaner. On the contrary, a true self that is busy with desires is dimmer and dirtier.

2. What/Who True Self Really Is

True self, as mentioned before, is the self that has been in existence even before our human self today and will continue to exist even after we have died, even after the end of time. Often times, to further explain who this "spark"/the part of us that will continue to exist even after the end of time is, people tend to use the spiritual terminology "children of God." We must be careful with this term because people usually use this term to refer to the whole part of us including the human part. Although our destiny is to return to our Source, our temporary physical body is just flesh and blood that will turn into dust. We must also remember that the Creator is the Most High, and we are merely the Creator's subjects. Even our true self does not reflect our similarities with the Creator. We are only a speck of dust; we matter only because there is Love from the Creator for us.

Chapter 5

TRUE SELF IN DIFFERENT PLACES

The true self that resides within our heart is actually only a small part of our true self. If the idea of our true self in several places simultaneously sounds incredible, just remember that we are not talking about a limited physical entity here. An analogy for a true self being in multiple places at once would be: we can pour water from one glass into multiple glasses; the water is still the same water; it is now simply in different places and of different quantity. Though our true self does not need a container like water needs a glass, our true self can certainly be in different places simultaneously.

Some true selves can be in the planning dimension, other dimensions, and many other places. However, knowing exactly where our true self is not the main point. We just need to know about our main true self in the Void and our true self that is in the school of spirits.

Our Main True Self in the Void

Our main true self is not the one that resides within our heart—this true self is only a small part. Our main true self resides beyond all dimensions, known as the Void.

All true selves are in the Void. The true self of every human and other beings that have true selves can be found in the Void. There is nothing but true selves and True Source's Blessing in the Void. Thus, it is a mistake to think that visions seen during meditation such as planets, buildings, or any other forms come from the Void.

All true selves in the Void are directly in front of True Source. No true self is behind another true self. No true self can hide behind another. There are true selves that are lower, farther from True Source, and they are smaller and dimmer than the true selves that are closer to True Source. The location and the condition of each true self do not reflect age, power, or knowledge of each true self; rather they reflect each true self's surrendering attitude to True Source.

Illustration 7 shows that:

o   all true selves are directly in front of the Creator. No true self is behind any other true selves.

o   true selves that are farther from the Creator are always smaller and dimmer compared to the true selves who are closer to the Creator.

Again, where a true self is and its condition are not based on its age, power, or even its knowledge. How close a true self is to the Creator and how big and how bright it is depend on how much each true self surrenders to the Creator.

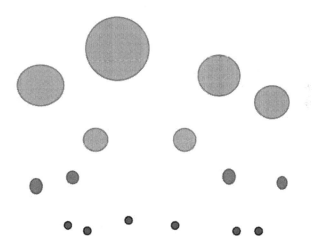

Illustration 7: true selves in the Void

The most important message after all of this information about our true self in the Void is: the location and the condition of a true self depends on how much each true self surrenders to the Creator. This is the KEY to spiritual progress (the progress of every spirit/true self).

With regard to the connection between our main true self in the Void and our true self within our heart, know that the small part of our true self within our heart helps our true self to learn the best from being in a physical human form and living life in this physical realm.

> "The location and condition of a true self are not based on its age, power, or even its knowledge. How close a true self is to the Creator and how big and how bright it is depend on how much each true self surrenders to the Creator."

The Spirit School

In addition to our main true self that is in front of the Creator in the Void, our true self is also in a special place that we shall refer to as the spirit school.

The class system in the spirit school is different from the earthly school that we know of in terms of who runs the classes and the going up and down the class levels.

o   A class is led by a main guide who is a student in a higher class (one level above). This main guide is also helped by several classmates.

o   Because the lessons are about realizations which are reflected in the attitude of the whole self, it is possible for true self to go up or down a level at any moment.

o   All true selves are in this school of spirits.

Spiritual Guides

A class is led by a true self who is also a student in a class (one level above). This true self has a better understanding of the lessons that are being learned by the class, but this true self has not understood or realized the lessons completely either, so guiding the class is actually a chance for this true self to get the best because through guiding other true selves and through seeing its own actions and reactions for every event, this true self can realize what needs to be realized.

This true self, who is the main guide of a class, is also helped by other true selves in guiding the class. These guides are also students in a class one level higher than the class being guided. The main guide and the helpers are classmates in their own class.

True selves that guide other true selves in the school of spirits are commonly known by humans as "spiritual guides." Every person has one main spiritual guide and several additional spiritual guides.

Many people are looking for their spiritual guides on earth with the hope of being able to learn directly from their spiritual guides because they want to progress spiritually. This is actually not a good idea for the following reasons:

- what the spiritual guides can teach us on earth has been taught to us in the spirit school
- the spiritual guides themselves have not completed the lessons; they themselves are still learning and are limited in what they know, understand, or realize.

Many people, in their enthusiastic quest to find their spiritual guides in this world, are learning about matters they consider spiritual from someone who is actually in a lower-level class in the spirit school. One can only imagine the consequences of doing that.

It is important to know that one main topic of the lessons given in the spirit school is: every true self has to follow his/her own Inner Heart because Inner Heart is the spark of True Source that receives direct guidance from True Source—this is beyond what any spiritual guide of any level can offer.

Realizations are the Lessons

In addition to the main lesson of using and following our Inner Heart, another set of lessons in the spirit school is usually closely related to the main lesson given in the planning dimension. A note on the planning dimension: our form in the planning dimension is our non-physical body with our soul as the center of consciousness as there is no true self in the planning dimension. Our guide in the planning dimension is usually the same guide we have in the spirit school.

In the planning dimension, our guide discussed with us important lessons that we need to learn, and based on our previous actions, we were given choices of different lives. More detailed information on the planning dimension can be read in <u>Spiritual Journey for the Ultimate Destiny</u>.

Recognizing the main lessons that were assigned to us in the planning dimension for this life is very important. Recognizing these lessons is actually not difficult; all we have to do is look at the "challenges" we experience in our daily life. By "challenges," I do not mean life adversities or worldly situations (things that are outside of ourselves), but our own traits, attitudes, and characteristics such as:

o   arrogance
o   anger
o   jealousy
o   irresponsibility
o   etc.

This is why we are given this life. This life is a facility to directly experience what needs to be learned so that our true self can get a more-complete and deeper understanding and realizations of the real lessons.

The condition of our true self/the attitude of our true self is a reflection of our realizations, and because our realizations are still limited, we end up going up or down the levels of classes in the spirit school. An example to illustrate our limited realization is: we all have experienced having been deeply touched by a piece of information that we know was important, and we made a promise to ourselves to be diligent in doing something based on that realization, yet, after a while, this attitude faded, and we stopped being diligent.

All True Selves are in the Spirit School.

All true selves who have not fulfilled their highest nature completely, regardless of their level, are in this spirit school without any exception. All true selves, except for those in the lowest class, are both students (in their own class) and guides (for the lower-level class) with main responsibilities, and sometimes they are also helped by classmates.

Chapter 6

THE JOURNEY OF OUR TRUE SELF

As has been discussed, true selves have been in existence for a long time. Some true selves are older than others, but regardless of our age, all of us are on earth for one purpose: to learn. Why do we need to learn? The answer is: we are learning so that we all can return completely to True Source.

> "The final purpose is to return completely to True Source."

Illustration 8 shows the journey of true self and how our soul and our lives on this earth fit in this journey. Our true self was the one that came into existence first, and for a while, there was only true self. It was not until the first life form that we were given a soul along with its non-physical layers for the purpose that has been explained in Chapter 2. Within our soul is our true self, and both are always together within our heart when we are still in our life form/still alive. When we die, our flesh-and-blood physical body returns to ash and dust, and what is left are the non-physical body layers that temporarily look identical to our physical body, with the soul as its center of consciousness and with true self within the soul. In holy books, we often hear about our souls being rewarded in heaven or punished in hell. Where is our true self during this time? It is together with the soul. If our soul goes to heaven, our true self is in heaven too. If our soul still has attachments and stays in a place where we have those attachments, then our true self within our soul is there too. If our soul goes to hell, our true self is there too.

However, please remember that the true self that is within our heart and within our soul (and in our physical body while we are still alive) is only a small part of our whole true self. Our main true self is always in the Void and all the while, our true self is also in the spirit school.

What happens to the main true self in the Void and in the spirit school upon death? To the true self in the Void and the true self in the spirit school, the termination of the physical form makes no difference.

Our state (alive or dead) does not affect our true self in the Void or in the school of spirits. Changes to true self in these places depend on the true self's attitude toward True Source.

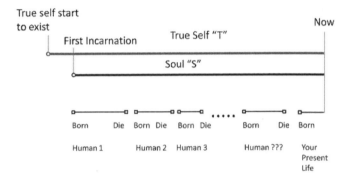

Illustration 8: journey of true self

You may have noticed that there are multiple life forms shown in Illustration 8. Our physical form is temporary, limited, and cannot function for a long time. The multiple life forms are given to us because time and again, we failed to use our lives according to True Source's Will, so we are given chance after chance to complete our lessons. Also, notice that I did not use the term "human" for each life because in addition to being born as a human of any race in any country on this planet, it is possible for a true self to be given a form of life that is not human. The form of life depends on what we have done in the past. An example would be: we can see how some babies were born into this world with good health with good surroundings, and there are babies born into this world with challenges and less-than-ideal surroundings. Even in human forms, each true self is given unique situations; these depend on what lessons we need to learn.

Regardless of what form we are in and what type of situation we find ourselves in, the most important thing is: how much are we using our life for the real purpose of life, which is to choose True Source and to get closer to True Source? This is why people say "Find lessons in everything." This understanding can be taken further: when we really realize that the real purpose of life is to get closer to True Source, we will use every situation to remember True Source, to open our heart to True Source, and to surrender to True Source. In addition to getting closer to True Source, remembering True Source, opening our heart to True Source, and surrendering to True Source means that we are accepting True Source's Blessing even better, and we let True Source's Blessing help and guide us in every situation.

Thus, every time our true self opens our heart and surrenders to True Source, True Source's Blessing does the most wonderful things on and for our true self, making us cleaner, brighter, and bigger and automatically we are getting closer to True Source. True Source's Blessing is available for all beings and opening our heart and surrendering to True Source improve all aspects of us.

On the contrary, if our true self is busy following our desires/our own ways, we are turning away from True Source. The busier and more emotional we are, the further our true self turns away from True Source. We are moving further away from True Source, and automatically, our true self becomes dirtier, smaller, and dimmer.

The condition of our true self is closely related to our heart attitude, which will be discussed later in this book. For those of you who have been guided to feel your heart and have started to open your heart and use your heart in your daily life, you should understand what I mean easily. Know that remembering True Source and wanting to get closer to True Source do not necessarily mean that our true self has the same attitude.

Illustration 9a shows how without using our heart, even though we are praying, our true self could be busy with itself or other matters.

*Illustration 9a: without using our heart, even though we are praying,
our true self could be busy with itself or other matters*

Again, the condition of our true self depends on our heart attitude, and this attitude changes all the time. Illustration 9b shows the change of our true self's attitude when we use our heart well. If we can continuously open and use our heart to prioritize True Source, we will continuously be brought closer to True Source.

*Illustration 9b: by using our heart properly, our true self has the
proper attitude according to True Source's Will*

Our true self in the spirit school is also experiencing all these attitudes. Because realizations/attitudes are the lessons, our true self can go up or down a class level in the spirit school. Because a true self's improvement is limited, it is not too easy for a true self to go up class levels; it takes an exceptionally good change to go to the higher level class. However, true selves whose attitudes continue to improve will go up to the next level. True selves who do not have good attitudes for a while can also go down a level in the spirit school.

As previously mentioned, the condition of a true self is not affected by the physical form. A person's realizations after he/she dies are usually the same as his/her realizations when he/she was still alive. Those who remember and choose the Creator in the busyness of life will remember the Creator too when they have passed away. Those who are always busy with worldly matters and did not have a chance to choose the Creator wholeheartedly are not able to choose the Creator after they have died. The only difference between before-and-after death is the existence of the physical body and the brain. The other two consciousnesses, the soul and true self, are still exactly the same. Our heart is also still the same heart. This is why it is often said everything that we have done is reflected in the condition of our heart.

The journey of true self continues on even after the person's death. To help true self improve its condition, another chance is given in the form of another life. In this subsequent life, the same true self gets another chance to choose True Source over his/her desires/ways/emotions until this true self can choose True Source completely to return to True Source completely. After a true self has completely returned to True Source, this true self will not change its attitude towards True Source, and the condition will not change. This true self is in the most beautiful place that True Source has provided.

The topic of reincarnation should not pose a problem to those who do not believe in reincarnation. Those who do not believe in reincarnation can use this life as the only life to embrace and accept True Source's Blessing, to surrender to True Source, and to be brought Home completely by True Source. All facilities have been given to attain the real purpose of existence. Inner Heart, heart, and life are Gifts of Love from True Source for everyone to be used the best way possible. By using our heart and Inner Heart, the special Gifts of Love that True Source has given us humans, we can be connected to True Source and embrace and accept True Source's Blessing according to True Source's Will.

Chapter 7

THE HUMAN FORM (WHY THE LIMITED PHYSICAL BODY)

In some holy books, it is clearly stated that human beings receive the highest priority from the Creator. Why did the Creator give us a physical body that is very limited? How can this limited physical form help our true self that is more remarkable than this human body?

I would like to share with you an understanding and a realization that many people and I obtained after we reached our true self consciousness where we re-experienced or remembered again the real experience before we were given this human body. As true selves that can do many things, do not get tired, and can not die, we are very busy. We have desires, and we are busy following all of our desires. Even before one desire has been fulfilled, more desires surface, making us extremely occupied with all of these never-ending desires.

Illustration 10a: we have the tendency to be busy

Because of our never-ending desires and busyness, our remarkable true self is given a human form that is full of limitations in ability, power, and even mortality.

With a limited human body that needs rest and sleep, we learn to stop. This limited physical form does not allow us to use our whole attention and our whole self (which means "use our heart") continuously for our needs/desires. Stopping our busyness is also important because it helps us to see how being continuously busy with desires is actually not enjoyable.

This limited physical form helps us to learn to enjoy moments when we are not busy. More importantly, stopping our busyness is an important step to be able to prioritize True Source. It helps us to remember True Source, to open our heart to True Source, and to surrender to True Source in prayers from our heart.

Our mortality helps us to realize that life is temporary, and it helps us to look for something eternal. In our search, we will remember True Source and will realize that only True Source and True Source's Blessings are beyond this life and eternal. Our mortality gives us a sweet excuse to be willing to be helped in realizing True Source's Greatness and True Source's Unlimited Love for us so that we can start opening our heart to True Source and have our heart be directed to True Source.

Imagine if we do not need to rest, to sleep, or that we cannot die. What would the whole world be like filled with immortal humans full of strong desires and busy with all of these never-ending strong desires?

Knowing that the purpose of our limitations and mortality is to help us realize that True Source is the Almighty and that True Source has Unlimited Love for us, we should make a conscious decision to choose True Source by stopping our busyness to surrender our whole heart and our whole self through prayers from the heart.

Stopping our busyness does not mean we do not do anything at all. Rather, it means we surrender our desires to True Source. To further illustrate the difference between following our desires and surrendering to True Source, let us do an experiment in the form of getting ready to pray with two different attitudes:

Make a list of two or three things that you hope for/that you need.

A. Get ready to pray to ask the Creator for all these things that you hope for/need.
B. Now, get ready to pray just to surrender more to True Source.

Are you able to feel the differences between A and B? Do you realize that there is relief and joy in B? If you are not able to feel the differences, repeat the two until you are able to feel them. If you are able to feel the differences at the first try, that means your heart and the feeling from your heart are quite strong already.

The above experiment is very simple. For those of you who were able to feel the differences, it should be clear that it is the different attitudes (A and B) for the same action (getting ready to pray) that produced the different results. The feeling that you experienced in A was the result of following your desires. The feeling you experienced in B was the result of surrendering to True Source.

To surrender to True Source, we need to open and use our heart. If you have ever tried to quieten your mind or have tried to calm yourself, you may have felt that there were some parts of you that were still busy. This busyness comes from our soul and our true self. Although our brain and our physical body stop our busyness, it does not mean that our true self stops too. The lessening of this busyness is still limited when our brain is the one in charge.

Even after we understand that we need to stop our busyness, stopping our busyness without using our heart is not good enough. It is not unusual for some people to have a lot of strong desires, and they are so busy with these desires that even when they are doing relaxed activities such as eating or resting, their thoughts and their whole selves are still filled with these strong desires. Even when they sleep, they are still busy. This is because without the proper use of our heart, our soul and our true self can still be busy (Illustration 10b).

Illustration 10b: without the proper use of our heart, even in our sleep, we can still be busy.

Those who have started to open their heart to True Source, use their heart in their daily life, surrender to True Source, and prioritize True Source have reported that their sleep has become peaceful (Illustration 11).

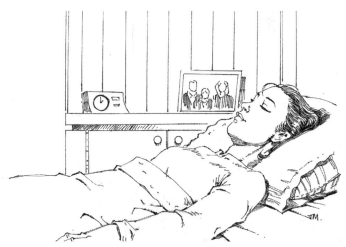

Illustration 11: with the proper use of our heart, surrendering to True Source, we sleep soundly and peacefully.

Again, stopping our busyness does not mean we do not take part in any life activities. We can do many things in life with the understanding that life is just a facility to get closer to True Source, to open our heart to True Source, to surrender to True Source, to prioritize True Source, and to ultimately return completely to True Source. If we remember that True Source loves us and has given us and continuously gives us abundant Blessings, with an open heart, True Source's Unlimited Blessing can help us in everything: freeing us from burdens, doing the most wonderful things on and for our true self, directing our true self to True Source, and bringing us closer to True Source.

Having worldly responsibilities does not mean we are unable to stop our busyness to prioritize True Source. We can start doing our daily activities including our tasks and responsibilities at our workplace just as beautiful facilities to surrender to True Source. In the "getting ready to pray" experiment, it should be clear that it is the attitude that matters because the action itself was the same. Understanding that this temporary life is a facility to remember, to choose, and to prioritize True Source, I present in this book the ways to improve the condition and the attitude of our true selves towards True Source. However, please remember that this can be done only after you are able to use your heart well, In Chapter 12, I will give you two basic heart exercises, and in Chapter 13, I will give you information about our Inner Heart. More detailed information can be read in <u>Smile to Your Heart Meditations</u> book and <u>Inner Heart</u> book.

Chapter 8

REINCARNATION
(MULTIPLE LIFE FORMS)

The debate over whether reincarnation is real or not can be put into the perspective of the bigger picture of the real purpose of life. Those who believe in reincarnation can use this life the best by understanding that they have failed continuously that they are now here in this life, given another chance to attain the real purpose of life. Let this life be the last life to reach the final destiny so that no further reincarnation is needed. Those who do not believe in reincarnations can use this life the best by understanding that this life is the only life that they have, and this life is the only chance that they have to fulfill their destiny to return to True Source completely by relying onto True Source's Blessing, opening their hearts to True Source, and surrendering to True Source.

As for the questioning of why some people have a good life and others do not, again, remember that life is only a facility for our true self to learn/realize what it needs to learn/realize. Before we are lost in the questioning of the fairness of life situations, we should remind ourselves that we can even be born as a non-human. Just as our human form is to serve a function, other forms of life are given to our true selves, also complete with their limitations and mortality, to help our true selves to learn to stop from being busy and to remember True Source. No matter what situations or conditions we are now in, remember that humans receive the highest priority from True Source. Life is a Blessing.

Because life is a facility for our true self to learn, life situations depend on the lessons that each true self needs to learn/realize. The journey of true self to reach the real purpose of existence is a long journey. In one or two lifetimes, it is possible for a true self to use these facilities (life forms) to improve its attitude toward True Source. However, if the final purpose has not been attained, true self will continue to be given facilities (life forms) over and over again until true self attains the final purpose, i.e. to return completely to True Source.

It is not enough to simply *know* about the lessons that true self needs to learn. A true self needs to really *realize* these lessons to the point that this realization is reflected in the attitude of the true self, i.e. choosing True Source completely by opening the heart and surrendering to True Source completely. We know that in life, we are still affected by our situations and surroundings. The limitation in our realization/attitude affects our true self's attitude toward True Source. Life is a beautiful facility to show us our weaknesses so that we realize how limited we are and how relying on True Source's Blessing is very beautiful.

Throughout our lifetimes, we have good attitude and bad attitude. This up-and-down pattern has been taking place in all life forms. For example, it is very possible that after a continuous improvement over several lifetimes, we suddenly took a big backward step because we were influenced by something in another life. This made the journey of our true self become longer.

Many people have asked: "Why weren't we given the memory of past lifetimes to make it easy for us in this lifetime, allowing us to simply continue what we have done in the past?"

It is not as simple as that. Keep in mind that we did not use many of our past lives properly. Imagine if we had to live this life based on the backward steps/our true self's bad attitude in the last life. Even if in our last life we did well, it is not about the past. We have to remember that every moment, including this moment in this lifetime, is a chance to choose True Source over ourselves. Rest assured that even though in this lifetime we do not remember the details from our past lives, the improvement that we obtained in past lives is reflected in our true self's condition and attitude toward True Source. There is no need to busy ourselves with wanting to know the details in our past lives because after all, no matter how much we improved in our past lives, obviously we had not reached the minimum level of relying on True Source's Blessing or we would not have been born in this lifetime. From here, it should be clear that it is not about knowing the details of our situations and surroundings of our past lives that is important, but it is really about choosing True Source, in any situation, wherever we are, and whatever role we play.

There is an obvious reason why our brain cannot remember the details of our past life experiences. How could our brain that never experienced all those things *remember* them? Our brain in this lifetime was given to us when we were in our mother's womb. The brain that went through the events in our past lives had turned into ash and dust at the end of each lifetime. As discussed in Soul Consciousness, it was our soul and true self that experienced our past lives. Also, as shown in Illustration 3a: *Layers of Consciousnesses in Humans*, our brain is the outermost layer and therefore is unable to access the higher consciousness deep within it that keep these memories.

Another reason why we were not given the memory of our past lives is that our brain would not be able to handle it. Our physical body is full of limitations. Our brain, as a part of our physical makeup, is also limited. It would be an excessive burden for our brain to have to deal with all of those memories of past lives, even if some of the memories were good. If we were given the memory of all that we experienced in the past, our brain would not be able to handle it.

It is true that some people are able to remember what took place in their past lives. Spiritually, without the proper preparation or practice, this is considered a "leak" from within where the higher consciousness leaks information to the outermost/surface consciousness that is the brain. As fascinating and exciting as it sounds, spiritually, this actually is not a good thing because we need to have the proper preparation and proper attitude so that all realizations or remembrance of past life events that we obtained from reaching our higher consciousness can be used the best way, which is only for the real purpose of life instead of for other purposes.

With the proper preparation, reviewing important matters from past lives can help us use this lifetime for the real purpose of life. Our weaknesses are usually repeated in many lifetimes, and most likely they still exist in this lifetime; it is just that we are not able to see/realize them prior to our reviewing our past lives by reaching our higher consciousness. Reviewing our weaknesses in our past lives will help us to recognize them more easily in this lifetime, and we can then rely on True Source's Blessing to take care of these weaknesses.

As shown in Illustration 2: *Soul: Archiving Experiences,* mistakes made in past lives caused defects in our soul. Realizing this is important, but what's more important is to remember that our own effort in trying to cleanse it or make it right is very limited and the best thing to do is to rely on True Source's Unlimited Blessing as that is what's best as the Blessing can take care of these matters.

This is only an example of the benefits of knowing about our past lives with the proper preparation. By "proper," I mean by simply relying on True Source's Blessing, allowing even the process of reaching a higher consciousness itself as a facility to surrender to True Source more completely.

Chapter 9

PSYCHIC ABILITIES

Most of us are very familiar only with our physical five senses; therefore, having or hearing psychic ability from the 6th sense and beyond can fascinate us. We know that the ability to see nonphysical matters, the ability to hear nonphysical things, and other psychic abilities exist. There is no denying that these things can be fascinating. However, now we know that our true self is much more remarkable and less limited than any or all of these psychic abilities combined. This is because psychic abilities are simply from the non-physical part of us whereas our true self is beyond non physical.

In my books and at workshops, I speak of these fascinating beyond-physical-realms matters, yet at the same time, I also discourage people from engaging in them. This is because when it comes to non-physical matters, there are many things that look similar on the surface that actually are very different. More importantly, the purposes may also look similar when actually they are very different.

I speak of these fascinating matters to relate them with the heart and Inner Heart because our heart and Inner Heart are very important, and using them is one of the keys in attaining the real purpose of life. We have discussed how one of true self's weaknesses is not using Inner Heart and not letting Inner Heart be the proper director. We also know how we are very limited and that we need to let True Source's Blessing help us in this matter. This whole life is for that. Therefore, while we are in this physical body, we need to use this life as a facility to learn/to work on our weaknesses and to get closer to True Source instead of being distracted by things that look fascinating but have purposes that take us away from the real purpose of life.

Admittedly, when I first started out more than a decade ago, while I was still searching by reading books and learning from spiritual authorities, I found psychic abilities fascinating. I also discussed all these findings in my earlier books. However, after I reached my true self consciousness and realized how True Source loves us completely and wants to always help us, I let go of all of those fascinating things, and I started reminding others about what I have just shared with you. Even in my books related to Reiki TUMMO channeling, I did not speak of having a special ability. Energy channeling is only a facility for us to remember True Source—how True Source always loves us and wants to give us the best. It is a matter of us remembering True Source, opening our heart to True Source, and surrendering to True Source, to accept True Source's Blessing that can help us to be healthy, calm, and peaceful, and of course to get closer to True Source.

With regard to psychic abilities, they are actually not as impressive as our heart and our Inner Heart. After all, remember that our soul and true self already know about these "fascinating" nonphysical matters/dimensions all along. Psychic abilities allow us to see only what is in the nonphysical dimensions below and above ours. Psychic abilities are still limited in the sense that they do not extend to being able to communicate with true self. Even those beings who are in the highest dimension are not able to communicate with true self. This is because true self is beyond nonphysical. As shown in Illustration 6b, divine matters such as true self and True Source's Blessings are beyond the nonphysical realm. The beings in the highest dimension can only see the radiation around True Source's Blessing. Our heart, on the other hand, is a special Gift of Love from True Source that houses our true self, the highest consciousness that is beyond nonphysical. Our heart, or more specifically, the core of our heart, the Inner Heart, has access not only to all of the nonphysical dimensions but also beyond. If beings from the highest dimension can see only the radiation around the Blessing, our heart and Inner Heart can feel and realize True Source's Blessing. Using our heart with Inner Heart as director, we can feel and realize about our true self.

Realizing this, it truly is a beautiful Gift of Love to be able to use our heart and Inner Heart, not to check or find out about nonphysical matters/dimensions out of mere curiosity, but to use our heart and Inner Heart only for the most important and the most beautiful purpose of all, which is to accept True Source's Blessing completely, to get closer to True Source, according to True Source's Will.

I always encourage everyone to use this life the best according to True Source's Will because the Most Loving True Source purposely gives us this physical form full of limitations in order for us to remember and choose True Source.

Chapter 10

TRUE SELF'S MAIN SHORTCOMING AND THE LESSONS ASSIGNED IN LIFE

We have already learned that our true self has never-ending desires and is continuously busy following these desires which means its heart, our Inner Heart, is directed toward these desires and thus is no longer directed toward True Source. Not using and not following Inner Heart properly is true self's main shortcoming that causes true self to move further and further away from True Source.

Had we allowed our Inner Heart to be the director properly and had we followed our Inner Heart every moment, our Inner Heart would have accepted True Source's Blessings completely, which means we would have returned to True Source completely.

In order for us to use this life as a facility for our true self to learn the best, we need to understand the connection between true self's main shortcoming with the lessons assigned in life.

What is the connection between arrogance, anger, envy, jealousy, and other negative emotions in our life with our true self not using Inner Heart?

This matter is so deep that even our soul and our true self do not recognize it. It is only because of True Source's Blessing that I was able to realize the connection between the lessons assigned in life and true self's main shortcoming. The three points below show you the sequence of the connection between them.

Completing a Lesson

From what we have experienced in life, we should be able to see that we are not able to rid ourselves of negative emotions *completely*. We are not even able to fully get rid of just *one* type of negative emotion. Of course, with age and life experiences, many older people no longer react with such intense negative emotions as young people do. However, even the least emotional person still has negative emotions be it anger, arrogance, envy, jealousy, and so on. Just because the negative emotion is not expressed does not mean that it is not there. As soon as a thought crosses our mind and the related negative emotion surfaces, even if they are not intense or are very mild, it means that we still have those negativities within us.

Negative traits within us have been with us for a very long time, and they are deep within us, within our true self. Even though we have been given chance after chance, going through life after life, and even if we have improved significantly, these negative traits are still within us as can be seen clearly in this life. It is obvious from the presence of these negative traits that we have not fully completed our main lessons.

Why have we not completed our lessons? Why can't we get rid of even *one* negative emotion within us? The answer is simple: we are limited beings, and we need to realize that True Source is the only one who can remove negativities completely from our brain, soul, and true self. All we have to do is accept it as a Gift of Love from True Source.

Life is full of facilities that tend to trigger us to react negatively. We need all these facilities so that we can realize what our weaknesses are and to not choose them but to choose True Source instead. Trying to control our negative emotions or trying to deal with them using our own ways also helps us to see and realize our limitations. Then, after we realize how we are very limited, we can start to rely on True Source's Blessing. It will become very clear to us how relying on True Source's Blessing is very beautiful and we will begin to see how everything can be different. All this is a beautiful facility to help us trust True Source more and to choose True Source more completely. We need to open our heart and accept True Source's Blessing completely.

Accepting Gifts of Love from True Source

We need to realize that the only way we can fully complete our lessons is by accepting the help from True Source only as a Blessing/ Gifts of Love. In order to accept True Source's Help/Blessing/Gifts of Love, we need to open and use the proper tool, which is our heart, the key connection to True Source.

Opening Our Heart Completely to True Source

Opening our heart to True Source is not difficult at all; however, our heart is very deep. Opening our heart completely to True Source means that the core of our heart, the Inner Heart, needs to also be opened.

For our whole self (our brain, soul, and even our true self) to accept the abundant Gifts of Love from True Source, our Inner Heart needs to be the director every moment. By having our Inner Heart as the director every moment, -

- everything related to the lessons discussed in the planning dimension that our soul accepted to do in this life,
- our true self's shortcoming,
- and the important things that we as humans need to do will become very clear, and our whole self will be directed to this same purpose

Relying on True Source's Blessing is actually one of our main lessons. However, this important lesson was missed by our souls in the planning dimension because we have the tendency to rely on ourselves instead of relying on True Source's Blessing. True Source is the last resort to many souls. We can also see many humans rely on many other matters before they remember True Source/ask for help from True Source.

This is why the human form has to go through major events in life to start to realize the importance and the beauty of relying on True Source's Blessing. Relying on True Source's Blessing is important not only in this life but also after this life ends because this is about the connection between our true self with True Source.

Now that we know our shortcomings and why we have been given life forms, we can start living this life the best for the real purpose. Let us open our heart and rely on True Source's Blessing and live our life only to open our heart and surrender to True Source more completely.

Chapter 11

USING THIS LIFE
(USING OUR HEART)

An advantage of our physical body, a beautiful Gift of Love from True Source, lies in its limitations. With our physical body, we are not able to be continuously busy with our wants and desires which if we continuously follow will direct our heart towards all those things, which means we are turning away from True Source. Our physical body is a very good facility to stop our busyness. Stopping our busyness helps us to remember True Source and to be grateful to True Source.

When we remember True Source often and are grateful to True Source more frequently, we are just starting to be on the path that True Source wants us to be. Why do I say that we are "just starting"? It is because we think we already remember True Source and are grateful to True Source properly when actually to be proper, we need to be wholehearted.

To know what whole*heart*ed means, we need to know what *heart* is.

Heart

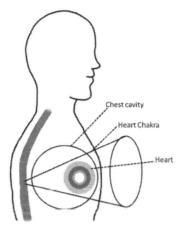

Illustration 12: our heart within

The "heart" we are referring to is not the physical heart but a non-physical heart (within our chest cavity) which is the center of gentle and beautiful feeling, where our true self, with a spark of True Source within it, resides.

Just as our ears were created to hear and our eyes were created to see, our heart was created to feel wonderful, gentle, beautiful feelings. However, if our ears, eyes, and other physical parts made of flesh and blood that will turn into dust have limited physical functions, our heart can recognize something beyond that no other part of us can recognize. Our heart recognizes True Source and True Source's Blessings.

Our heart is the only one that can recognize divine matters because within our heart is our true self and Inner Heart, the spark of True Source that can recognize True Source and True Source's Blessing. This is why our heart is the key connection to True Source.

Without using our heart in praying, being grateful, and other matters related to True Source, what we do is very limited as we do these things from our brain. It is only through the use of our heart that we can be properly connected to True Source and can communicate with True Source according to True Source's Will. Because our physical body is temporary and everything we do in life is only a facility to improve the connection between our true self and True Source, we need to use our heart.

Using our heart properly while we are still alive in this human form is the key to be connected to True Source. It is important to understand the connection between life and the use of our heart. Using our heart means we are living this life for the real purpose of life, which is to improve the connection between our true self with True Source, to surrender to True Source, and ultimately, to return to True Source completely.

Heart is a special Gift of Love from True Source for us humans. Our heart is the only tool that can be connected to True Source. Using our heart is the only way to use our life as a facility for our true self. Please remember that we cannot do anything to our true self; only True Source's Help and Blessing can do the most wonderful things to our true self, and our heart is that tool that helps us accept True Source's Help and Blessings.

> "Our heart is the only one that can recognize divine matters because within our heart is our true self and Inner Heart, the spark of True Source that can recognize True Source and True Source's Blessing. This is why our heart is the key connection to True Source."

Because our heart is a very special Gift of Love from True Source, only True Source's Blessings can access our heart, and in order to cleanse, open, or use our heart, we need to always rely on the Blessings. Moments when we use our heart properly are moments when we let True Source's Blessings help our true self.

As soon as we use our heart for matters related to our connection to True Source, the true self within our heart and everywhere else automatically does these things simultaneously. As soon as our heart embraces and accepts True Source's Blessings, our true self everywhere also embraces and accepts True Source's Blessings. When our heart chooses True Source completely and we let True Source's Blessings do the best, our true self in the spirit school can improve rapidly and can go to the next class several times with no limit in just one lifetime. This is very beautiful. Using our heart is the key that we need to understand to be able to use our life according to its real purpose

Only by using our heart properly can our true self rely on True Source's Blessing. By using our heart properly, our true self becomes less busy, becomes more directed to True Source, prioritizes True Source more, and relies on True Source's Blessing, which means our true self's connection to True Source improves. The human part of us will clearly feel the calmness, peace, and joy from the improvement of our true self's connection with True Source. We will also be able to feel this clear and beautiful connection. The beauty and the joy of True Source's Blessing will fill our whole heart and our whole self.

Are We Using Our Heart?

Have we used our heart? Are we using our heart? Why do I introduce Strengthening of the Heart exercise and Open Heart Meditation to others? Why do all of my books of different topics emphasize the importance of opening and using our heart to improve our connection to True Source? Have people not used their hearts already?

Many people believe that they are already using their hearts. Some of the things they said:

"If I did not use my heart, I would not be praying."

"If I did not use my heart, I would not be able to feel peace and calmness when I pray."

"If I did not use my heart, why would I want to pray routinely?"

Rather that immediately responding to the comments above, let me share with you first what some people are saying after they attended Open Heart workshops:

> Using my heart has changed my prayer life. I am now able
> to feel and experience the Love within my heart, as well as
> my spiritual connection to the Creator, the True Source.
> Praying from the heart—not just with words—allows me
> to feel and be grateful for the many blessings received; helps
> me to surrender my problems to, and rely on the Creator's

Love to work on my heart and life; and helps me to realize the importance of forgiving and asking for forgiveness.

At home, being within my heart helps me to smile and be more joyful when interacting with family members. (It also changes doing housework, which in the past caused resentment). Caring for family members by sharing the Creator's Love is so wonderful, as interactions from the heart with loved ones are now gentler, more patient, and more loving.

The way of experiencing and using the heart is the most joyful and wonderful way to live—sharing the Love with others, and loving our Creator, the True Source, more and more.

Sally Mydlowec, Executive Vice President and Dean of Academic Affairs, Pennsylvania, PA

Opening the heart . . . discovering I even HAD a heart . . . has been a miraculous gift beyond anything this world has already given me . . . or could give me.

Opening the heart opens your eyes so that you can truly see . . . everything . . . everything that we have already been given, but couldn't see. It's a bit like getting those 3-D glasses and seeing the depth of life for the first time. I saw through eyes controlled by my brain for most of my life . . . labelling and judging everything, every situation, worrying endlessly about things I needed to get done, (or things I had forgotten to do!), and then with this beautiful gift came insight deeper than the deepest ocean. Now, I feel more like that ocean . . . with life's dramas becoming like ripples on the surface so different to the stormy seas they use to be. And the sight that's been given—that incredible blessing—has helped me see the truth of all things more clearly . . . the truth of people, who we really are beyond our stories, who we all are beyond this life.

THE REAL YOU: BEYOND FORMS AND LIVES

I only wish these words could capture a fragment of the meaning that has arrived since my heart has been opened... like an impossibly beautiful dream. I feel such incredible gratitude. The Source of Love and Light is here and now all around us. All we have to do is open the door and say 'Welcome!' :):):)

Steve Ray
Melbourne, Australia

Sometimes you feel like you have been searching your whole life for something, and you don't even know it until you find it. That is the way it was for me when I met my own heart.

I knew that I was longing for a feeling of Home and a connection with the Creator through which I could just be me and be loved and love in return, no matter what. I had a sense that this was what our adventure on earth was all about. I already knew that what I longed for wasn't in being successful, having a loving relationship, being attractive, having children or a beautiful house. As nice as these all are they require a lot of feeding, and the results are often uncertain.

I meditated for 32 years, and taught meditation to others. I listened to and spoke inspiring words. I met people who seemed to have what I was looking for, but found they were not able to pass it onto me. I tried to give up and settle for less, but I got depressed and felt even more empty and lost than before. After traveling through the lessons of two marriages, step-parenthood, and a career as a psychologist, a friend of mine told me what he had learned through a gifted teacher. That the key to our connection Home is the heart, not the physical muscle that pumps our blood, but the non physical heart that we talk about when we say "follow your heart" or "a pure heart".

It is the heart that you pick up and dial and then listen to in order to connect back again to the feelings of love, calmness, and joy. I had been trying for years to get to those feelings through a peaceful mind, which hadn't worked very well. I thought if your mind was quiet enough then what was underneath the mental chatter would be love and joy. What I found was that a lot of calm mind could get pretty boring, and that it was hard work keeping it calm even some of the time when living a normal life. That is why most people seeking to quiet the mind usually had to go to a retreat place to find it. At times, I had tried to use my head to connect with my heart by focusing on being loving or visualizing being loved. What I hadn't realized was that I had to go directly to the heart, not through any other part of me, in order to be able to feel what is within it, Divine Love and Light.

It has been three years since I first began experiencing and enjoying the feelings from my heart, feelings gentle, beautiful, sweet and powerful at the same time, beyond anything I could have imagined. All my good feelings had always been coming from there, I had just not known how to access them. More wonderful still, I now experience that the heart is the key to our connection with our Creator, the Divine Source, which is why the wonderful feelings are there, not in our heads. Being in our hearts leads to a life lived in love, which leads us closer and closer to our true Home and destiny as human beings, to our Creator.

How wonderful it is for me to be able to say that this is no longer a far off dream or something written about in a holy book, but something that is available now.

Diana Stone, Ph.D
North Carolina, U.S.A.

I have never been taught how to open my heart and go into my heart in my many years as a priest and a missionary. By opening my heart, I am able to feel, enjoy, and be grateful for

God's ever-present Love which is a blessing for both myself and the congregation that I serve.

~ *Fr. Ignatius Sudaryanto, CICM, a Catholic priest, Head of the Regional Asian CICM Seminary* ~

As a spiritual aspirant for over 30 years, and in my profession as a Ph.D. psychologist, I have experienced and taught numerous practices and approaches for enhancing wellbeing and spiritual growth.

In these, I used to believe I knew about being in my heart, and did not realize that I was still primarily head-centered. I spent countless hours doing disciplined meditation practices, and could easily experience the calm space between my thoughts. However, with all of those practices, I never got to experience the depth of my heart. I have come to realize that mindfulness is not the same as "heartfulness."

If we reflect back to the most special times in which we felt so deeply touched, grateful, and connected to life—whether that was the birth of a child, a tranquil moment in nature, a peak experience, or time of spiritual communion—it was our heart that was touched. In that moment, we were connected with our heart, and that is why it felt so special and precious.

Over the entire span of a person's life, when all is said and done, and when one is about to leave this earthly plane, it is these few heartfelt experiences that give them their greatest sense of satisfaction and joy.

My happiness comes from the realization that our heart is not reserved for just a handful of special moments. We are meant to live *as a heart*, so that every moment can be special and precious, and so life is filled with abundant love and joy.

When our hearts are open, we become less and less bothered by idiosyncrasies or differences in people. Relationships begin to bring great joy; we become more accepting of our shortcomings, as well as others'; we easily forgive, and share from our heart.

The quality of life improves as people realize that what used to push their buttons, or create emotional reactivity, no longer does so. And if negativity is triggered, it is significantly diminished compared to previous patterns. They feel more sweetness and joy in their relationships, and allow the intelligence of the heart to guide their lives.

Open hearts live authentically with love, humbleness, and gratitude. And the more that we are able to open our hearts, the more we are able to experience a tangible connection to the Source of Love and Light.

I am so happy that I know from the core of my heart that this is something reachable and achievable for all of us. It is our birthright. I am so grateful that True Source is supporting us to fulfill this ultimate destiny.

Ed Rubenstein, Ph.D.
North Carolina, U.S.A

From what they shared, I hope that you can see that they were able to feel the difference after they have opened and used their hearts. For now, let us first look at the connection between Divine Love and the use of our heart.

Love and the Use of Heart

I have been referring to the Divine Love as "Blessing" instead of "love" because Divine Love is more commonly known as blessing instead of love. I refrained from using the word love because some people have interpreted the word love using a worldly point of view, which is the love between humans which is actually impure and contains emotions.

When it comes to Divine Love, the difference between the word "Blessing" and the word "Love" lies in the understanding and the attitude of the recipients. A simple analogy is: two people are given identical items; Person One accepts the item as if it was his/her right to get that item and he/she is not grateful upon receiving the item whereas Person Two accepts the item as a beautiful and valuable gift with much appreciation/gratitude, and he/she feels joyful for having received the gift. The item is the same, but the attitudes of the recipients are different.

Also, spiritually speaking, many people's hearts perceive "Blessing" as a thing/an object whereas the word "Love" reminds their hearts that it is the "feeling"/Love from True Source for them. The explanation on these two words is not intended as a theoretical discussion on terminology but serves as an introduction to show the connection between Divine Love/True Source's Love and the use of our heart.

To feel True Source's Love and the beauty of the Love, again, only by using our heart can we really feel True Source's Love and the beauty of the Love. True Source's Love is gentle and beautiful, so when we use our heart, we are filled with this gentle, beautiful feeling of Love. If we are tense and emotional when we talk about the Love, clearly we are not filled with Love but with our own thoughts and concepts that we label as "Love." Judging others is also a clear indication that we are not being filled with Love because being judgmental is not a characteristic of Love. Love is gentle, forgiving, loving, and so on.

Knowing the characteristics of Love can help us to recognize and feel the benefits of using our heart and to accept and experience the real Divine Love. Every time we use our heart, we are filled with all the beautiful feelings/characteristics of Love. If we have not felt that we are filled with all of these beautiful feelings, it means we are still using our heart in a limited way.

> "It is clear that when we are tense and emotional, even when we are thinking of talking about Love, we are not being filled with Love but filled with our own thoughts and concepts that we label as 'Love.'"

I will now respond to the answers that people gave me about their belief that they were already using their hearts.

"If I did not use my heart, I would not be praying." In our daily life, we use our brain to think, speak, and do many other actions. In the act of praying, we also tend to use our brain. Concentrating on our prayer or being solemn in our prayers do not guarantee that we are using our heart properly. Concentrating on our prayer means we are concentrating on our prayer. Being solemn in our prayers means we really do intend to pray well. Without having experienced the feeling from our heart/without using our heart properly, chances are we are still using our brain even when we pray to the Creator because we have been using our brain all the time in doing all kinds of activities every moment of our life.

In our daily life, our brain is dominant and therefore our heart is caged, not free, and is not used even in the act of praying which is actually about connecting to True Source. One indication when our heart is strong and free is when we are joyful. However, we are not always joyful in our life, and even when we are joyful, it could be more emotional happiness that is also still from the brain instead of the pure joy from the feeling from our heart. For example, laughing happily is not the same as experiencing gentle feeling that is filling our heart and self. Many people associate surface happiness with feeling from the heart when actually feeling from the heart is light, gentle, and beautiful. Only by being diligent in our practice of using our heart can we recognize the true feeling from our heart and improve the way we use our heart in our daily life, including and especially in the act of praying to the Creator.

"If I did not use my heart, I would not be able to feel peace and calmness when I pray." There is a marked difference between the peace and calmness praying from the brain and the beautiful feeling in praying from the heart that needs to be experienced by the prayers themselves. With the proper use of our heart, when we pray or call out to True Source, we will feel the prayer from our heart as a beautiful feeling filling our heart, moving upward, and we can feel the beauty of our Love connection with True Source. The beauty of being connected and praying to True Source can be felt clearly in each prayer from the heart.

"If I did not use my heart, why would I want to pray routinely?" Our dedication and commitment in wanting to get closer to True Source do not always come solely from our heart. The Creator gave us this physical body complete with our brain so that our brain can also recognize the importance of choosing the Creator, the Help, and the Blessings, so it is very possible that this commitment and dedication come from our brain. The main difference between praying routinely from our brain and from our heart is that when we use our heart in praying, longing for True Source will surface. This longing is also not emotional but gentle and beautiful.

Because the purpose of all of my books is to realize the real purpose of life and to open our heart to True Source to rely on True Source's Blessings and to surrender to True Source, two basic foundations in using our heart, namely Strengthening of the Heart exercise and Open Heart Meditation are given in this book. Further tips and details on how to use our heart properly can be read in Smile to Your Heart Meditations book.

Chapter 12

STEPS IN STRENGTHENING AND USING OUR HEART

Below is a brief explanation on how you can start to strengthen and use your heart.

Strengthening Your Heart

Though simple, this exercise is very important and very useful in helping your heart to be stronger. This Strengthening Your Heart exercise helps to have our attention be on our heart, lessen the brain's domination, and strengthen your heart and your feeling from the heart.

You can record the step-by-step instruction below and listen to it so that you can close your eyes; because reading the steps or memorizing and then trying to recall the steps, will prevent you from relaxing completely.

Find a peaceful place to do this Strengthening of Your Heart exercise. You can sit on a chair or on the floor depending on what you are more comfortable with. If you sit on a chair, ensure that the seat is not too soft so that your whole body can be quite still as you do this. Keep your spine straight without tensing yourself—having a straight-backed chair and sitting as closely as possible to the back part of the chair would help achieve this.

Strengthening Your Heart Exercise:

1. Relax so that your brain relaxes more
2. Close your eyes to further decrease the activities of your brain
3. Touch your heart with one or two fingers

4. Smile freely to your heart without thinking how or where
5. With your eyes closed, stay relaxed and keep on smiling to your heart {about 1 minute}. Stay relaxed even though you have thoughts coming in; just don't follow your thoughts. Stay relaxed.
6. You will feel an expanding/calm/peaceful/light or joyful feeling in your chest
7. This wonderful feeling indicates that your heart is starting to work. Follow this wonderful feeling without observing it to let your heart and the feeling from your heart to become stronger.
8. If you haven't felt anything, continue to relax and smile; you don't have to do anything. When you stop looking or trying, you will start to feel the wonderful feeling. Keep on relaxing and smiling freely.
9. As soon as you feel the wonderful feeling, follow this nice feeling while continuing to relax and smiling freely. Enjoy . . . {2 minutes + }

Open Heart Prayer

In addition to strengthening your heart routinely, do also the Open Heart Prayer. We have a lot of negativities within us from all the negative emotions that have accumulated in our heart for many years. These negativities need to be removed to make space for True Source's Blessings.

Only True Source's Blessings can open our heart; thus, we rely on True Source's Blessings by praying. Just like in Strengthening of the Heart exercise, find a peaceful place to do this Open Heart Prayer, sit straight without tensing yourself, and relax and smile.

The main part of opening our heart to the Creator is to pray to the Creator. In order to pray to True Source from our heart, we will take some steps to prepare our heart properly. The combination of this heart preparation and the Open Heart Prayer is called Open Heart Meditation.

Even though it is called "meditation," Open Heart Meditation is very different from what is commonly known as meditation in the sense that:

1. We do not want to "empty" ourselves. We want to relax, but we do not want to be empty because being empty/vacant/ lost is not good in any exercise.
2. We rely on True Source's Blessings completely.

Open Heart Meditation CD and Open Heart Meditation booklet can be obtained from Padmacahaya branches in your local area. Contact information is in the Appendix of this book.

- Sit in a relaxed position . . . with your spine straight without tensing yourself . . . .
- Place both palms on your lap facing upward . . . .
- Close your eyes to lessen the activities of your brain . . . .
- Relax . . . . and smile . . . . Let yourself be here and now completely . . . to do this Open Heart Meditation the best way possible . . . .
- Continuing to relax and smile . . . . inhale deeply without forcing yourself . . . . and exhale through your mouth . . . . letting all thoughts and burdens to leave you with every exhalation . . . . and feel you are becoming more relaxed . . . feel and enjoy moments when your whole self is becoming more relaxed . . . . and smile more freely . . . .
- Inhale deeply . . . . and exhale from your mouth . . . . letting all tension on your whole body leave you with every exhalation . . . . and feel your whole body is becoming more relaxed too . . . . Feel . . . . and enjoy moments when your whole self is becoming more and more relaxed . . . . and smile even more freely . . . .
- Inhale deeply . . . . and exhale through your mouth . . . . let the rest of your thoughts and tension leave you with every exhalation . . . . and now feel how your thoughts and whole body are becoming very relaxed . . . . Enjoy . . . and smile

as you enjoy moments you are relaxed . . . . and breathe normally through your nose . . . .

- Now . . . . touch the center of your chest with one or two fingers, touching your heart . . . . and smile to your heart without thinking about it or looking where your heart is . . . . keep on smiling freely . . . .
- Keep on smiling freely to your heart . . . with all of your feeling . . . . Feel that you are becoming calmer . . . . Enjoy . . . . while smiling . . . . in moments like these, you are letting your heart become stronger . . . .
- While continuing to touch your heart and smiling to your heart and enjoying the calmness from your heart, let us now ask for Blessings from the Creator so that the emotions within our heart can be cleansed and for our heart to open more to the Creator. When praying, you do not need to repeat the prayer lines. Simply let your heart pray as that is the best way to pray.

  o *True Source, please bless our heart . . . so that all arrogance be replaced with Your Blessings*
  o *True Source, please bless our heart . . . so that all anger be replaced with Your Blessings*
  o *True Source, please bless our heart . . . so that all selfishness be replaced with Your Blessings*
  o *True Source, please bless our heart . . . so that all envy and jealousy be replaced with Your Blessing*
  o *True Source, please bless our heart . . . so that all cunningness and greediness be replaced with Your Blessings*
  o *True Source, please help us to realize that our heart is the key connection to You . . . we need to keep our heart clean because our connection to You is the most important . . . please bless and help us to be able to forgive others . . . . sincerely . . . .*
  o *{now . . . forgive everyone who has done you wrong . . . including those who are still hurting you . . . remember that*

69

*your connection to True Source is the most important . . .
(1 minute)}*

o   *True Source . . . by having forgiven everyone who has done
wrong to us . . . please bless our heart so that all hatred,
grudges, hurt feelings, dissatisfaction and other negative
emotions be removed from our heart to be replaced with
Your Blessings*

o   *True Source . . . . please bless and help us to be able to
realize all of our wrongdoings to You and to others . . . . for
us to regret and ask for Your Forgiveness sincerely . . . .*

o   *{now . . . realize all of your wrongdoings to True Source
and to others . . . regret them and ask forTrue Source's
forgiveness . . . . (1 minute)}*

o   *True Source . . . please forgive all of our wrongdoings to You
or to others . . .*

o   *Having our wrongdoings be forgiven by You, please bless
for all burdens, fear, worries, and other negative emotions
be removed from our whole heart and replaced with Your
Blessings*

o   *True Source, please bless our heart so all worries and fears
caused by the lack of trust in You be cleansed and replaced
with Your Blessings*

o   *True Source . . . with the negative emotions removed
from our heart, please bless our heart to be more open to
You . . . . and to be more directed toward You . . . . and for
Your Blessing to flow more abundantly into our heart . . . .
so that our feeling from our heart becomes stronger . . . . so
that we can feel calmness . . . . peace . . . . and the beauty of
Your Blessing even better . . . .*

o   *True Source . . . . may Your Blessing fill our whole heart and
our whole self . . . so that our whole heart and our whole
self can be filled with calmness . . . and peace . . . . so that
we can rely onto Your Blessing . . . . to always be within our
heart . . . . and to be within Your Blessing . . . .*

o *True Source . . . . we thank You for Your Love that has cleansed the negative emotions from our heart and self . . . . that has opened and directed our heart even better to You . . . . so that our whole heart and our whole self are filled with Your Blessing . . . . so that we can feel and enjoy calmness . . . . peace . . . . and beauty of Your Love even better . . . .*

o *Thank You, True Source . . . . Amen . . . .*

- Continuing to touch your heart and smiling, feel how your whole heart and your whole self have become lighter . . . . enjoy . . . . and stay within this peace and calmness . . . . this is the time when you are within your heart . . . . Keep on smiling and enjoying . . . .
- While smiling and enjoying, let yourself go deeper and dissolve in the peace and calmness from True Source's Blessings and dissolve even more into the Blessing . . . . Feel . . . . the more dissolved you are in this peace and calmness, the lighter and the more beautiful your feeling is. Enjoy . . . .
- Continuing to smile while enjoying the peace, the calmness, and the beauty of True Source's Love, slowly move your fingers, and open your eyes with a happy smile.
- Live your daily life staying within your heart—within the peace and the calmness from True Source's Love.

Notes:
1. **The Open Heart Prayer is an example of asking for True Source's Blessings to remove negative emotions within us. You may use terminology or words that you are comfortable with.**
2. **This Open Heart Prayer is not meant to replace your other prayers.**
3. **For the best results, do this Open Heart Meditation twice a day. When you do Open Heart Meditation in the morning,**

you will start the day with a calmer, lighter, and more peaceful heart, and this will help you throughout the day. Do the Open Heart Meditation once more in the afternoon or at night after you have gone through the day so that all of your excessive thoughts and burdens can be cleansed. You will feel calmer and more peaceful. You will sleep more soundly and wake up fresher the next day.

If you do not have time to do Open Heart Meditation twice a day, doing it once a day regularly for some time would also give you benefits. You will feel that your heart and self are calmer, lighter and more peaceful in your daily life.

Detailed information and various heart exercises to strengthen, open, and use your heart can be found in <u>Smile to Your Heart Meditations</u> book.

Chapter 13

INNER HEART

As previously explained and as shown in Illustration 5, within our heart is our true self, and within our true self is the core of our heart, our Inner Heart.

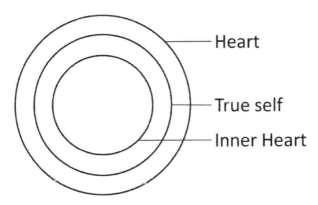

Illustration 13: Inner Heart: the core of our heart and true self

Just as a human should use the heart, true self should also use its heart (the Inner Heart) because Inner Heart is the spark of True Source and is the only part of true self that can recognize True Source's Love, True Source's Will, and True Source. Without using our Inner Heart and without having Inner Heart as the director, all other parts of us including our soul and true self will continue to function with limitations.

Spiritually speaking, as imperfect beings, it is impossible for us to do the best. No matter how good our understanding is, there are still limitations, mistakes, and shortcomings from our part. For example, the understanding that there are countless problems in the world and the belief that the Creator is the Almighty are analyzed by some people as such: "Yes, the Almighty Creator exists, but this world is vast, and there are too many things in this world; the Creator does not take care of every single thing; this is why there are still problems, crimes, and even wars in this world." However, there was a mistake in that analysis because "The Almighty" part was not taken into account. To say that this world is too vast for the Almighty Creator reminds us that sometimes our limited brain forgets that it is limited in its way of working and in its knowledge. This is only an example of how a brain may analyze and make a deduction to fit what seems logical to that brain. It is clear that there are still mistakes made because of our limitations.

In our limitations, we forget that we are very limited. We forget that we do not know everything. If the whole truth and all facts are like a giant puzzle made of millions of puzzle pieces, we have only several puzzle pieces, yet we try to use our limited number of puzzle pieces to describe the giant, complete picture.

This is why there are various opinions or even contradictory points of view on one single truth. Each person/group focuses on certain puzzle pieces that are often discussed, analyzed, and even taken into smaller pieces to describe the giant, complete picture. Each person/group often "forgets" or does not even know about other puzzle pieces, so those are not taken into account at all. This happens all the time.

We used to think that the earth was flat and that the sun revolved around our earth. The fact and the real truth were discovered much later. This simple example shows us how we could believe something to be the truth when it is not; this proves our limitation.

The examples given so far illustrate the limitation of our brain. However, it is not only our brain that is limited. Our soul and our true self are also limited. This means our soul and our true self can still make mistakes too.

Even though our soul and true self know much more than our brain, they still do not know everything, especially when it comes to matters related to True Source and the Real Truth, i.e. True Source's Will. Communicating with or reaching our soul consciousness or true self consciousness is not the way to find out how to get closer to True Source or discover True Source's Will. Our soul and true self can give extensive information on countless matters, but they cannot give the best when it comes to how to get closer to True Source.

If we understand that this life is a facility to get closer to True Source, we will realize that many fascinating things are actually not important and that getting closer to True Source is most important. If communicating with or reaching soul consciousness and true self consciousness is still the most important thing to us, it also means that we do not understand that both of our higher consciousnesses are limited. This is very important.

Once we feel that realizing the real truth beyond our limitations, i.e. realizing True Source's Will and getting closer to True Source and living our lives according to the real purpose are important, we will then realize that using our Inner Heart is the only answer.

Illustration 9a in Chapter 6 actually also shows that a true self that does not use its heart (our Inner Heart) still has a limited connection with True Source. Remember that one main shortcoming of our true self is that it does not use Inner Heart properly. This is why even though our physical body is already doing the best when praying (even if it includes prostrating), it is very possible that our true self in our heart, in the Void, in the spirit school, and everywhere else is still busy with other matters. By taking the first step, which is to strengthen, open and use our heart, our heart will be more directed to True Source and will become cleaner and stronger.

Using our heart is a beautiful beginning step, and it is true that the proper use of our heart helps our true self to also be directed to True Source and our true self would choose True Source too. However, in addition to using our heart properly, we also need to use our Inner Heart. Without the proper use of Inner Heart as the director of our whole heart and our whole self, the use of our heart would still be limited. There is a simple way to understand the importance of using our Inner Heart and why I said using our heart is only a beginning step. We cannot claim that we have opened and used our heart completely if the core of our heart—our Inner Heart—is not used properly. Opening and using our heart completely means that we need to also use the core of our heart, i.e. our Inner Heart.

> "Without the proper use of Inner Heart as the director of our whole heart and our whole self, the use of our heart would still be limited.
>
> We cannot claim that we have opened and used our heart completely if the core of our heart—our Inner Heart—is not used properly. Opening and using our heart completely means that we need to also use the core of our heart, i.e. our Inner Heart."

Without our Inner Heart as a director, even with dedication and commitment and the proper use of our heart, it would take many years to be able use our heart every moment of our life. How many hours a day can we really use our heart? What about the remaining hours of the day?

To go beyond our heart's limitations and to further improve our connection with True Source, in addition to using our heart properly, we need to also use our Inner Heart because the longing within our Inner Heart helps us to prioritize True Source and accept all of True Source's Most Beautiful Gifts of Love that will bring us to True Source completely. This longing from our Inner Heart is the one that continues to choose and be directed to True Source.

With Inner Heart as the director, in addition to having our true self everywhere pray to True Source when the rest of us prays (Illustration 9b), the longing from our Inner Heart will continue to choose and be directed to True Source beyond the several hours of the day when our physical body and thoughts choose to use our heart. The use of Inner Heart as the proper director of our whole heart and our whole self means that our true self is also starting to use its Heart. When our true self uses Inner Heart, the connection between our true self and True Source improves significantly.

This longing for True Source that is felt by our true self can also be felt by our heart. When we use the core of our heart, our whole heart and even our whole self can also feel the longing clearly. This helps us to want to use our heart and Inner Heart more often in our daily life, not because we have to but because of the beautiful, natural longing from our Inner Heart for True Source.

Chapter 14

USING OUR INNER HEART

The best and most proper way to use our Inner Heart is by letting True Source's Blessing help us so that our Inner Heart becomes the director of our whole true self, soul, and even our brain. In this book, I give a general overview of the steps needed to let Inner Heart become the director of the whole heart and whole self after the opening and using or the heart. Using our Inner Heart as the director is very deep. We can let the Blessing help our Inner Heart to become the proper director only after we have opened and used our heart properly and can let ourselves be very deep within our heart, beyond all of the impurities within our heart, all the way to the clean part that is near our Inner Heart.

Please remember that I always say, "Let True Source's Blessing help." This is not mere lip service. Always remember that True Source's Blessing is the only one that can cleanse, open, and direct our heart to True Source. Only True Source's Blessing can do everything else related to the heart and especially the deeper part of our heart, down to the core of our heart, our Inner Heart. Only True Source's Blessing can help our Inner Heart become the proper director of our whole heart and our whole self.

Realizing that True Source's Blessing is the only one that can help us in this matter, relying on True Source's Blessing in everything that we do becomes very beautiful. This attitude will help us to open our heart more and to surrender to True Source more. When we open our heart and surrender to True Source more, our connection to True Source improves.

Again, using our Inner Heart as the director is very deep. We can let the Blessing help our Inner Heart to become the proper director only after we have opened and used our heart properly and can let ourselves be very deep within our heart, beyond all of the impurities within our heart, all the way to the clean part that is near our Inner Heart.

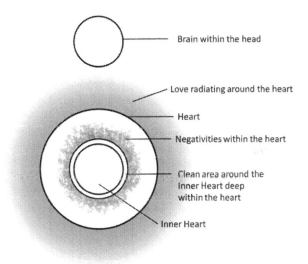

Illustration 14: from our brain to the area near our Inner Heart

The first step is to have our heart opened and used properly, i.e. having our heart be directed to True Source and accept True Source's Blessing until the Blessing fills our heart and radiates beyond the border of our heart. If you are sensitive, you should be able to feel the nice, light, gentle, beautiful feeling filling up your chest and radiating toward all directions. The sensation may be in and around your chest area.

The next step is to let True Source's Blessing bring you into the Blessing. If you are sensitive, you should be able to feel that the beautiful feeling is no longer only in and around your chest area but is all around you.

There are more steps that you have to go through in order to use your Inner Heart because your Inner Heart is very deep. After opening and using our heart properly and letting True Source's Blessing bring us into the Blessing, we still need to let the Blessing bring us into our heart, and then into the deeper part of our heart near our Inner Heart, beyond the impurities within our heart. Finally, we can let True Source's Blessing help us so that our Inner Heart can become the proper director.

Although I make it sound simple and I keep it brief, this process is actually very deep. This is what I teach in Open Heart workshops and Inner Heart workshops. I guide the workshop participants step by step so that they can understand how to let True Source's Blessing help in every step. The method is natural because everything is about relying onTrue Source's Blessings.

Chapter 15

DO WE NEED TO
KNOW OUR OWN TRUE SELF?

We need to know our true self not to obtain information from it but to realize the real purpose of life. We know that the main reason our true self was given a limited physical body is to learn. Our need of physical rest and sleep helps us to stop our busyness, and our mortality gives us a chance to look for something eternal. Upon realizing the real purpose of life, we can choose to start to open and use our heart. Opening and using our heart help us to better realize the real purpose of life that helps us to start living our lives as a facility to get closer to True Source. After we have opened and used our heart properly, we will also use the core of heart, our Inner Heart, until it becomes the proper director of our whole heart and our whole self, which takes care of our true self's weaknesses and allows our true self to choose True Source and let True Source's Blessing bring our true self closer to True Source every moment.

Realizing the real purpose of life is different from understanding it. For example, we know that there are things that we are supposed to do, but if we do not really realize the importance of these things, we do not do them. There are many important matters that true self has not understood or realized. Our true self that has been in existence for a very long time needs this limited physical body to realize what it needs to realize. Knowing that our true self is still learning will help us to use this life for its real purpose.

Realizing that our true self still has not understood or has not realized important matters means that we do not need to learn from our true self. There is no need to try to get information from our true self because the knowledge has already been ours because our true self is a part of us. What we need to know is the weakness of our true self and that this physical body and life are a facility to let True Source's Blessing help us to remember True Source's Love for us, to be grateful to True Source, and to choose True Source more completely by opening our heart to True Source.

Realizing that one of the main weaknesses of our true self is that it does not use its heart, in addition to opening our heart to True Source, to further improve our connection with True Source, we need to use the core of our heart, our Inner Heart. We need to let the Blessing help us until our Inner Heart becomes the director of our whole heart and our whole self. Once we use our heart with Inner Heart as director, the longing from our Inner Heart will direct us to True Source.

The next step would be to realize that our Inner Heart is a spark of True Source. This is because without realizing that the core of our heart is a spark of True Source and only by using our heart with Inner Heart as the director, even with continuous longing for True Source, there are still borders and limitations. Without realizing that our Inner Heart is a spark of True Source, our true self, after allowing True Source's Blessing to bring us closer to True Source, upon reaching a certain distance will stop because we feel unworthy to be close to True Source. Because the most natural and highest nature of our true self is to return to True Source completely, it is not good to have this border because this is not according True Source's Will.

Without realizing that our Inner Heart is a spark of True Source, our true self will continue to have bad attitude towards True Source and will continue to function with limitations with regards to our connection to True Source. Our true self will continue to keep a distance with True Source, will continue to prioritize our own desires, and will not be able to trust True Source completely.

Again, understanding this is very different from realizing this using your heart and Inner Heart. It is by realizing that the core of our true self, our Inner Heart, is the spark of True Source would our true self's attitude toward True Source changes.

As soon as our true self realizes that Inner Heart is a spark of True Source, true self's attitude towards True Source improves. Only by realizing this can our true self really realize the real meaning and the real beauty of returning completely to True Source. This is why to fulfill our destiny of returning to True Source completely, we need to realize the meaning of our Inner Heart as a spark of True Source. Attaining this realization requires all of the consciousnesses, namely, true self, soul, and brain, to simultaneously prioritize and choose True Source completely, after the person has reached his/her true self consciousness. Reaching true self consciousness/being aware as a true self is needed for this realization to take place.

Chapter 16

TRUE SELF AND THE PURPOSE OF LIFE (ATTAINING THE REAL PURPOSE OF LIFE)

Topics discussed in this chapter are a summary of the previous chapters. All of the topics in the previous chapters are very deep, and it is natural to put extra attention on certain things that you find interesting or those that answer the questions you have been asking. This chapter is to point out the important matters related to the real purpose of life.

This life is meaningful and beautiful as Life is a direct Gift of Love from True Source for each one of us. This is why it is very important to use our life properly according to its real purpose.

Our true self is who we really are. Our true self is very old and has been in existence for a very long time. Our true self is unlimited, cannot get sick, and will not die—we could call it 'powerful' in our human language. However, our true self has too many desires and is always very busy following these desires, going from one to the next even before the first one has been fulfilled. This makes us forget about True Source, turn away from True Source, and eventually move further and further away from True Source.

This is why True Source gave us (our true self) this limited physical body with limited brain as the center of its consciousness. Because of its limitations, our physical body can do only certain, limited things too. Our physical body needs to eat, rest, and sleep—we are given a chance to stop our busyness so that we cannot follow our desires continuously. Because of the connection between our true self and our physical body, when our physical body stops when we rest or sleep, our true self also cannot continue to be completely busy following its desires. We also know that we will die; this helps our brain to look for something eternal—this makes us look for True Source and True Source's Love.

After we have found True Source and started to realize related important matters, we would stop not only when we have to or when we need to. We would gladly stop our busyness because we choose True Source by allocating time in our daily life to pray from our heart to True Source and by being grateful to True Source. Being grateful to True Source is extremely important because that is when our heart and our self are directed even more to True Source, admitting that everything that is beautiful comes from True Source.

Yet, even that is still not enough. We need to use our heart properly. Our heart is the key to our true self. When we use our heart, we are connected to our true self and by relying on True Source's Blessing in using our heart, our true self chooses True Source more, and it is more directed to True Source. While our brain takes the first step to remember True Source and to choose to open and use our heart, our heart is the one that is the key connection to True Source.

For the best result, we need to use our heart properly to the point where we also use the core of our heart, our Inner Heart, to be the director of our whole heart and our whole self. Using our Inner Heart means our true self is also using its heart; this is something that we should have always done but have not—this is one of our main weaknesses. We need to use our Inner Heart because only Inner Heart has longing for True Source. Only Inner Heart can realize True Source's Will. By using our heart and Inner Heart the best and as often as possible in our life and doing things in our life only as a facility to get closer to True Source, we can let True Source's Blessings bring us closer to True Source every moment.

In addition to using our heart with Inner Heart as director, we also need to realize that Inner Heart is a spark of True Source and the meaning because this helps our true self to realize the meaning and beauty of returning completely to True Source.

Heart is the First Key

By now you should be able to see the clear relationship between our heart, our true self, and our life. If we do not use our heart well enough, we are not using our life for the real purpose. If we do not open our heart to True Source, we worsen the condition of our true self because we dirty our heart with negative thoughts and emotions. Every single negative thought/emotion dirties our heart and negatively affects our true self's attitude toward True Source. The more we follow negative emotions, the more impurities and negativities accumulate in our heart, affecting our true self negatively.

The connection between our heart and our true self is very special. Whatever is happening on our heart directly affects the condition of our true self /our true self's attitude toward True Source. If we have burdens in our heart, for sure the following are taking place:

- our heart is not open good enough for True Source
- our heart is not directed good enough toward True Source
- our true self turns around/is no longer directed toward True Source
- our true self is moving further away from True Source
- our true self is not accepting True Source's Blessings and Help

By "burdens," I do not mean only heavy burdens. Burdens can be anything from any type of negative emotion or any excessive desire. Whether the burden is big, small, one type of emotion, many types of emotions, and so on, this burden affects the condition of our heart and our true self directly.

Be aware of how often we place burdens on our heart in our daily life which also means the placement of burdens on our true self. How many kinds of negative emotions do we experience in our daily life? How much desire, even for the simplest things in life, do we have? When we have negative emotions and too many desires, even for the simplest things in life, we place burdens on our heart.

When good and beautiful things are happening on our heart, these good and beautiful things are also happening on our true self. For example, when we are strengthening and opening our heart to True Source by relying on True Source's Blessings, it will help:

o   our heart to be more open to True Source
o   our heart to be more directed to True Source
o   our heart to accept True Source's Blessing
o   our true self to be directed even better to True Source
o   our true self to better accept True Source's Help and Blessings
o   our true self to get closer to True Source.

This is why in all of my books of various titles and topics I always emphasize the importance of strengthening our heart and opening our heart to True Source. Whatever we do on this earth, whatever role we play, all of these are just facilities for one thing: to bring us closer to True Source, to return us completely to True Source. Everything we do in life should be for this.

To improve on this, remember that True Source loves us completely. All we have to do is rely on True Source's Blessing every moment. For example, when a thought occurs and it is making us angry, we can instantly surrender this thought and the related emotion to True Source so that True Source's Blessing can remove them beautifully. When done properly, we progress spiritually because we remember True Source and we rely on True Source's Blessing with our heart. Also, remember that True Source's Blessing is most beautiful, complete, and perfect. When we rely on True Source's Blessing for one matter, because True Source is the Most Loving, True Source's Blessing is helping us in all matters.

In addition to using our heart to rely on True Source's Blessing to help us, we also need to open our heart to True Source and use our heart in everything that we do in life, every moment. For example, we need to understand and realize that doing good deeds/giving charity from the brain without the use of our heart with the core of our true self/the Inner Heart as the director does not improve the condition of our true self. Once we are able to tell the difference between using our brain and using our heart, we can start doing good deeds/giving charity from our heart. It will be clear to you how doing good deeds and giving charity from the brain are very limited and not related to the real purpose of life. Doing good deeds and giving charity from our heart is related to the real purpose of life because it improves the condition of our true self.

Our true self is the one that will continue to exist long after our brain disappears. Our true self even continues to exist beyond time. I invite your heart to realize this afterlife matters.

Realizing that using our heart improves the condition of our true self and our connection to True Source, I invite you to use your heart as you live this life. Again, our whole life and everything we do in life are only a facility for our true self to get closer to True Source, and we have been given the tool to improve our connection to True Source, i.e. our heart and Inner Heart.

Everything we do in this life is only a facility to let True Source's Blessing help us to improve our connection, i.e. the connection between our true self and True Source, with the ultimate destiny of returning completely to True Source. Let us show our gratitude for this life, a beautiful Gift of Love from True Source by using our life properly according to the real purpose of life. Life is a facility to get closer to True Source, to return completely to True Source, not by following our way, not with our hopes, but by relying on True Source's Blessings and following the Path that has been provided by True Source.

Life and Doing Everything for True Source

We should be very grateful to True Source because now we know the real purpose of life. However, it is not good to live our life *for* the purpose of life because when we do many things in life with the intention to return to True Source completely, it means we *want* it for ourselves. Desire is very deep. In this book, I discuss desire only to this point. Just remember again that one of true self's weaknesses is that we have too many never-ending desires. This is why to live our life for the purpose of life is still not good.

After we realize the real purpose of life, we surrender our desires to True Source about living our life for the real purpose of life, and we rely on True Source's Blessing to help us realize that to return completely to True Source is True Source's Will.

The real purpose of life is not for us. The real purpose of life is what True Source wants to happen on us. We should live and do everything in life not for our desires but with the realization that this is important, beautiful, and that it is True Source's Will. Only True Source's Will gives the best. Our best intention can cause us to have the wrong attitude. When it comes to the real purpose of life, we simply continue to rely on True Source's Blessing that is helping us to open our heart, direct our heart toward True Source, surrender our desires, and many other wonderful things related to this important and beautiful realization.

Chapter 17

COMMON MISCONCEPTIONS

In this chapter, common misconceptions about true selves are discussed. Some of these misconceptions are related to:

- seeing true self
- communicating with true self
- experiences during meditation
- reaching true self consciousness

Seeing True Self

True self is not the same as soul. If soul can still be seen by psychics, true self is beyond non-physical matters. Thus, we cannot see true self the way we see soul or other non-physical matters. True self does not have a form and can be recognized only by our heart or Inner Heart.

Communicating with True Self

Some people still believe that they need to obtain important information from their true selves. They try to make a connection with their true selves and the most common method is called "channeling."

In communicating with true self, intention alone is not enough. To use a phone-call analogy: it is not enough to pick up the receiver and think about the person we want to call to get connected directly with that person. We need to know the phone number, and we need to dial the number properly in order to be connected. People who obtain interesting information mistake the information as coming from true self when actually most of the information comes from their own subconsciousness, from their own brain, or from other beings.

To connect to our true self, the opening of the heart is needed because true self resides within the heart. It is only when a human has opened his/her heart properly and is already connected to his/her heart properly that the connection with true self is established.

Experiences during Meditations

Some people mistake their experiences during meditations as true self experiences. Some people have reported reaching their true self consciousness and meeting other true selves in various forms in a beautiful place. Please remember that all true selves are in the VOID and there are no beautiful sceneries, and there are no forms such as hermits or any other forms in the VOID. Thus, the experience of meeting a powerful hermit or any other form in a beautiful place cannot possibly be a true self experience. This type of experience is more likely an experience from soul consciousness because in soul consciousness, forms still exist even though they are nonphysical. At the level of soul consciousness, it is very possible to visit nonphysical places and meet nonphysical beings. Also, know that experiences of soul consciousness can also be mistaken. It is important to differentiate visualizations/imagination, subconsciousness, and an experience from the real soul consciousness too.

Some people have also shared stories about their meditation experiences where they felt that they reached a place with nothing but lights everywhere, and they consider this as the VOID. In addition, they also felt that they were very big as if they were unlimited and that the lights they saw were within them. This experience is good because it means some limitations around these people have disappeared, allowing them to feel as if there are no more borders. We do create borders around us that separate us not only from our surroundings but also from True Source's Blessing. By meditating, these borders/limitations dissipate; however, this does not mean that we are everything. This type of experience during meditation means that the person is better connected to the physical universe. On the journey of surrendering completely to True Source, when one returns completely to True Source, all borders and limitations disappear. Again, the main keys are:

o   only True Source's Blessing can give the best

o   we have to be in surrendering attitude to True Source.

The best meditation is a meditation to surrender to True Source. Even if we do not go through interesting experiences during meditation, if we meditate just to surrender more to True Source, it is the best meditation because it is for the real purpose. In contrast, if we enjoy going through interesting experiences during meditation, we need to ask ourselves what it is that we are looking for. Are we looking for mere interesting experiences or should we live our lives every moment to get closer to True Source?

If you would like to get closer to True Source, the best way to do it is by surrendering your whole heart and your whole self with your heart opening to True Source. In the journey/exercise, you may come across interesting experiences but please remember that if you choose to follow/ prioritize those interesting experiences, it means that your heart and your self are no longer completely directed to True Source. I invite you to let True Source's Blessing give you the most important thing in the afterlife: to be directed completely to True Source in surrendering our heart and self True Source.

Reaching True Self Consciousness

If you are interested in or are doing special exercises/practices to be able to shift to your true self consciousness, please remember:

o   your true self is within your heart

o   only True Source's Blessing can work on your heart.

Thus, everything we do or any technique we use in our attempt to reach our true self consciousness without the use of our heart and without relying on True Source's Blessing will not work.

You can reach your true self consciousness only if you open your heart to True Source and only if you rely on True Source's Blessing for the process to take place. You also need to know what true self consciousness really is. In your attempt to reach your true self consciousness, make sure you do not end up going into your subconsciousness or soul consciousness.

Being Possessed

Being possessed is very different from reaching a higher consciousness. A person who is possessed has another soul entering him/her, and his/her body is being controlled by this other soul consciousness. Being possessed has nothing to do with reaching a higher consciousness even though the consciousness that enters and controls the physical body is not a physical consciousness.

It is impossible to claim that the person being possessed is in his/her higher consciousness for this simple fact: that person is being controlled by another being. It is true that the person being possessed can give interesting information, but again, being possessed is not reaching a higher consciousness, and spiritually, this is not progress. The soul possessing the human body has not gone to a place that True Source has provided for it. This soul is still floating around, which means this soul has not realized something important, which is, after its physical body died, this soul must surrender to True Source to be brought to the best place for it.

Many Bodies, One True Self

Each human body has only one soul and only one true self. Each soul has only one true self. However, it is possible for one soul (with one true self within it because a true self is always within a soul) to have more than one body. Although it is rare, it is possible for one soul to be born in different places and to live multiple lives simultaneously.

Chapter 18

TRUE SELF PROGRAM

Below is additional information on the true self consciousness program from Padmacahaya International Institute of Inner Study.

True Self Consciousness Program

Illustration 15 shows the curriculum from Padmacahaya to reach true self consciousness. The beginning level starts with Open Heart Workshops level 1 to 6 where workshop participants learn to open and use their hearts until they are able to use Inner Heart as the proper director.

At the next level, each participant learns about his/her own true self journey and the real purpose of life by realizing these important matters using his/her own Inner Heart, allowing matters that were questioned or doubted to be felt and clarified by Inner Heart as this realization is beyond what can be obtained from reading or listening to others.

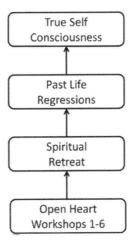

Illustration 15 Padmacahaya's Curriculum

Afterwards, with a strong heart and Inner Heart as better director, participants rely on True Source's Blessing to shift consciousness. Reaching the soul consciousness is the next step in relying on True Source's Love more completely and as a preparation to reach true self consciousness. Finally, reaching true self consciousness helps participants to realize that Inner Heart is the spark of True Source and to experience choosing and prioritizing True Source as they realize the beauty and the meaning of returning completely to True Source.

Rather than having you read other people's experiences about reaching their true self consciousness in this book, because this is very deep and it is much more beautiful and meaningful if you experience this journey yourself, I will share only one general testimonial about reaching true self consciousness for now. There are thousands of testimonials from others who have reached their true self consciousness, but again, something as deep and meaningful as this needs to be directly experienced to make it real.

> Opening my heart felt wonderful like a chink of light being
> let into somewhere I hadn't even realised was in the dark.

It got better and better with each additional workshop and exercises bringing better understandings, more peace, calmness and joy.

And then I had the opportunity to attain my True Self Consciousness. I cannot even begin to explain how wonderful it was. And I was and am so so grateful for the chance.

Before, my connection to True Source was defined by me by my concept of True Source, a picture in my mind, a feeling of distance, great respect but very much in the distance.

After attaining my True Self Consciousness, I felt and continue to feel the Love of True Source for me and for all beings not as a concept but in reality. I felt and continue to feel the connection, the individual, personal, close, loving connection I and all beings have with True Source and the gratitude for the chance to attain True Self Consciousness to feel the Love and to realise how much we are loved every moment always and the gift that is this life.

In my interaction with other people, it is easier to stay with the big picture, that all is well, that we are all Loved completely that we are all equally Loved completely and that we are all here together, in this time on this wonderful journey being helped and Loved every moment. In a practical way this means that I don't feel stressed as I did before. I am happy and calm, and my interactions with others around and those I meet are also happy and calm. This is equally the case for those close to me my family as it is for friends, work colleagues and aquaintances.

Attaining True Self Consciousness is a wonderful wonderful opportunity and your heart longs for the remembrance and joy it brings.

Geraldine Tobin
Ireland

Appendix 1

To find information on Open Heart Workshops worldwide, visit:
www.openheartmeditation.org
www.heartsanctuary.org
openheartworkshops.com

Related Books
by Irmansyah Effendi, M.Sc.

Smile To Your Heart: Simple Meditations for Peace, Health and Spiritual Growth (Ulysses), 2010

Sweet Heart (a children's book about the heart) 2007

Inner Heart (an updated and revised edition in English will be published soon)

Spiritual Journey for the Ultimate Destiny (a new and upcoming book)

About the Author

Since 1998, Irmansyah Effendi has been teaching workshops to help others use their own hearts and Inner Hearts as well as reach their soul consciousness and spirit/true self consciousness by relying on and surrendering to the Divine Source.

Irman has published 12 books, and his audience reaches all corners of the world with his workshops regularly conducted in cities in Asia, Australia, New Zealand, Europe, USA, Canada, South America, and South Africa.

17976426R00065

Made in the USA
Lexington, KY
10 October 2012